The Equine Listenology Guide

Horse books for adults

The Equine Listenology Guide
Dressage for Beginners
The Listenology Guide to Bitless Bridles
Ozzie, the Story of a Young Horse
Conversations with the Horse
Horse Anatomy Colouring Book

Horse books for kids

Listenology for Kids age 8-14
P is for Pony – The ABC Alphabet Book for kids 2+
Horse Care, Riding and Training for kids 6-11
Horse Puzzles, Games & Brain Teasers for kids 7-14

The Coral Cove Series for kids

The Riding School Connemara Pony
The Storm and the Connemara Pony
The Surprise Puppy and the Connemara Pony
The Castle Charity Ride and the Connemara Pony

The Connemara Adventure Series for kids

The Forgotten Horse
The Show Horse
The Mayfield Horse
The Stolen Horse
The Adventure Horse
The Lost Horse

The Equine Listenology Guide

Elaine Heney

First Edition May 2021

Illustrations by Faye Hobson

Editing by Kas Fitzpatrick

Published by Grey Pony Films

www.greyponyfilms.com

About Elaine Heney

Elaine Heney is an Irish horsewoman, film producer at Grey Pony Films, #1 best-selling author, and director of the award-winning 'Listening to the Horse™' documentary. She has helped over 120,000+ horse owners in 113 countries to create awesome relationships with their horses. Elaine's mission is to make the world a better place for the horse. She lives in Ireland with her horses Ozzie & Matilda.

Online horse training courses

Discover our series of world-renowned online groundwork, riding, training programs and iPhone and Android apps. Visit Grey Pony Films & learn more: www.greyponyfilms.com

Discover all Elaine's books at www.elaineheneybooks.com

Contents

Directing a documentary

5am in Orlando, Florida

It was Monday, November 12th, 2018 in Orlando, Florida. I woke up abruptly at 4.30am, drenched in a cold sweat. Waves of anxiety had been pouring off me all night. Sleep had been elusive. I could already feel the nerves starting to gather in the pit of my stomach. The hotel room was pitch dark, the only noise being the whirl of the air conditioning.

My suitcase with it's Dublin flight tags was lying in the corner of my room. Outside my window the Florida sun wasn't scheduled to rise for another 90 minutes. As I rolled out of bed it felt like the whole world was asleep and I was the only soul awake. I turned on the room light, got dressed quickly, walked to the wooden table and sat down in front of my laptop.

Today was going to be one of the most important days in my life. And there were just 28 minutes left to go.

I took a deep breath as my computer monitor flicked into life. Soon thousands of computers around the world would be tuning in. I started to feel physically sick with anxiety.

I looked over at the clock on the wall. It said 4.40am. Just 20 minutes to wait.

I logged into the website and double checked that everything looked ok. The registration page was working. Episode 1 was scheduled to start playing at 5am.

Thankfully during the few hours I had slept there had been no major technical incidents. So far so good. It looked like the last few moments of my plan was working.

15 minutes left to go.

I checked my emails. About 40 emails had come in overnight, a mixture of lost tickets and time zone confusion. I replied to all of them, confirming the launch time and sending out new invitations where needed. Another little step on this crazy project was completed.

I stood up, pushed back my chair and walked over to turn the kettle on. It would be the first of many cups of green tea that day. I noticed that my breathing had gotten faster. I looked at the clock as my stomach clenched with anxiety yet again.

Now there were just 5 minutes to go. Time seemed to have gotten faster too. Outside the world was in darkness. Aside from my laptop whirling and the sound of the fan, there was silence in the room. My palms started to feel sweaty as I stared for the last few moments at the computer screen.

Then, just like that, the small clock on my computer screen changed to 05:00am.

I watched as tens of thousands of emails were sent to homes around the world. Each email contained an invitation to watch day 1 of the top secret project that I had spent months working on without any sleep - working 24/7 to bring it to life.

Now it was the moment of truth.

The whole world would decide what would happen next...

Horses in Ireland

I had probably better introduce myself. I'm Elaine Heney and I live in Ireland. I sat on a pony for the first time at 6 years of age, to my great delight, and promptly fell in love with equines.

I spent many years growing up having fun with ponies. My family has always had horses too. Both my parents rode and my Dad in particular always had a young horse which he would 'bring on'. 'Bringing on' is the Irish term for building confidence, introducing a saddle and bridle for the first time, doing their first rides and developing them into a happy riding horse. The whole process would take about three to four years.

My grandad had a theory that you should be able to ride your horse with two pieces of silk thread - instead of using normal reins. Your cues should be that small and subtle that riding with a silk thread could be possible.

As I was growing up I understood that it was necessary to always be patient and kind with the horse, treat them with consideration and look at life from a horse's perspective. So my horse riding dreams - even from a young age - were BIG. I wanted to have a happy and confident riding horse. But I also wanted to go even further.

- I wanted to be able to do some of those fancy dressage moves I saw pictures of in horse magazines.
- I wanted to help my horse stay healthy well into old age.
- I wanted to build a partnership with my horse, so they connected to me as much as I connected to them.

While my Dad taught me all of the most important principles of being with a horse from when I was very young, he wasn't able to teach me the advanced dressage manoeuvres I wanted to learn. I had these crazy dreams of half-passing (a fancy type of sideways movement) across an Irish field with a beautifully balanced horse and swans flying overhead! As a teenager I was sent out to the larger world to get some traditional 'horse riding' lessons, to help me achieve my dressage goals. That's when things started to go wrong.

- "Pull her head in more."
- "You need to get her more on the bit".
- "You need to get her 'in a frame'."
- "Actually, you just need a *stronger bit.*"
- "Nope, that doesn't work, you need a double bridle (with 2 bits)."
- "That doesn't work. OK, you need to borrow a different horse."

So many technical terms were thrown at me that I didn't understand, let alone know how to achieve with my horse. Every beautiful dream I had as a child of having a gorgeous riding horse, seemed to disappear out of my reach. I got confused, I got stressed and anxious. The more I tried to do - using stronger hands on the reins, pulling on them a bit more to ask my horse to bring her nose in - just resulted in a more worried and stressed horse and a more worried and stressed me!

The more I tried to improve the worse everything got. It felt totally wrong. It wasn't fair to my horse. She did not deserve all this force and pressure. I felt so guilty that I had put her through these lessons. So I retired from all competitions and professional lessons at the ripe old age of 23. I felt like a failure in the horse world. I was obviously the wrong person, with the wrong horse, for all these beautiful dressage goals I had! For a few years we did trail rides at home, but I had no plan. I had lost my path.

I still had goals. I still wanted to be a kind horsewoman who was able to develop that light, soft and amazing riding horse without any gadgets or force. However I had no idea if something like that was even possible. I had convinced myself that I just wasn't a good enough rider (or maybe a tough enough rider) to be able to ride a 'fancy horse', doing fancy manoeuvres.

The Australian adventure

After a few years in my first office job in Dublin city I decided the time had come to go backpacking around Australia with some friends. It was the best decision ever.

I spent nearly three months travelling around Melbourne, Adelaide, Alice Springs, Uluru and Sydney. I took a flight up to Brisbane, on the east coast of Australia. Twelve weeks into my great Australian adventure I had a major issue. I'm a horse person, and after so many weeks of backpacking I was having serious withdrawal symptoms! I walked into an internet cafe in Brisbane and asked for an hour's web access. I sat down at a desktop computer and typed in www.google.com. Then I started researching websites of horse treks in Australia and New Zealand.

Anything to get near to a horse again!

I made a short list of about 25 horse treks, and wrote an email to each one, explaining who I was and asking if they had any horse trekking jobs available. Most people didn't reply and the ones who wrote back to me were already full.

Then an email arrived into my inbox that would change my life. It was from Mt. Lyford Horse Treks in New Zealand, which was about two hours north of Canterbury. They needed a trail guide for their trek business, which involved bringing tourists on horseback around the Southern Alps. They offered me a job as a trek guide in exchange for room and board. It sounded perfect. I would get to spend time with horses again - I was so excited! I booked a flight from Brisbane that evening, and arrived over two days later.

When I arrived at Mt. Lyford I had NO idea what to expect. I knew pretty much nothing about their horse treks, aside from having some lovely pictures of horses and mountains on the website. In fact, it was a wonderful place. All the horses they had there were beautifully cared for and lived together in what I can only describe as paradise on the South Island of New Zealand. But what really astonished me was that all the horses they had there were ridden in rope halters.

I had never seen a rope halter in my life! And I had certainly never considered using a rope halter, with no bit, to take out tourists. Many of them had never ridden before, and we were out exploring the southern Alps.

A rope halter is simply a halter or headcollar made out of a long piece of rope. The reins are usually another piece of thicker rope. When I was growing up in Ireland a halter or headcollar was something you put on a horse if you wanted to lead him somewhere on foot. It was not something you would use to ride in during lessons - and certainly not up a mountain!

The whole thing did not sound like a good idea to me. How wrong I was!

Over the three months I was there all the tourists were safe and happy. All the horses were happy and healthy. It was one of the most wonderful places to work in the world.

Then one day something really astonished me. The lead trail guide - who was a wonderful horsewoman - was riding her chestnut horse in a rope halter. But she was only using one rein. That blew my mind.

What she was doing was remarkable. She was cantering her horse, bareback, in a rope halter with one rein and her horse was totally relaxed and completely collected. My previously held belief that collection was only something that could be achieved with force and pressure was completely shattered. Not only could collection be achieved in a kind way, but you didn't need a saddle, you didn't need a bit and if you wanted to, it looked like you only needed one rein!

So my whole world shifted 110 degrees.

A new path to incredible horsemanship - that was kind to the horse, without using any force or gadgets - had just presented itself right in front of me. I literally soaked up everything I could learn there. I started emailing more people and on my way back home to Ireland I spent a wonderful week in Australia expanding my knowledge in Caboolture.

Eight months after I first landed in Australia on my backpacking trip, I flew home with a new mission. That mission was to restart my horsemanship education - but this time using gentle and kind ways to work with horses and to begin riding in one of these wonderful rope halters.

I wanted to learn as much as I could - and that's where the trouble began...

Trips to England

When I got back home to Ireland I realised no one was teaching this approach to horsemanship there, so I started Googling. Late one night, on an international horse forum based in England, I found out that there were people over there learning what I wanted to learn. Every year they were flying in trainers from around the world who would teach this horsemanship at clinics around the UK.

I flew to England to watch some of these clinics, and ended up learning as much as I could, travelling as much as I could manage. I became a sponge - I'd learn, then go home and try it out on my horses. I was also teaching students and their horses. I started to host clinics, bringing amazing trainers like Mark Rashid and Steve Halfpenny to Ireland. I ended up creating this amazing bubble for myself, and I got to know a lot of amazing horse people all over the world. My skills were improving, my understanding and partnership with my horses was improving too.

However there was still a problem. What I was doing wasn't the common approach in Ireland. While we do have lots of kind and talented horse people here, it was also common to visit local events and see some gadgets and tie-downs, stressed out and tense horses, and all of the stuff I really hate seeing. I believe that every horse deserves to be treated with kindness and patience - but this wasn't always what I was seeing in the real world.

So I decided to do something a little crazy. I decided to create a documentary that would promote the concept of listening to the

Horse, and I'd ask seventy of the most inspiring horse teachers and clinicians and friends of mine to share their experiences with the world. Then I would premiere this documentary online. So people could watch it no matter what country they were in - from Canada and the USA, over to Ireland and all the way around to Australia, South Africa and New Zealand.

That is how I ended up waking up at 4.30am in the hotel room in Orlando.

I had no idea what would happen.

From 5am to 5.45am on that Monday morning, horse owners from all around the world began watching episode 1.

Then at 5.45am, the emails started to flow into my inbox. In fact, they continued coming in all week and for many weeks and months after. The feedback was astonishing.

I was getting emails and stories and messages on every social media platform you can think of, from people sharing how much this documentary had helped them.

There were horse owners who had decided not to ride their three year olds until they were older. There were riders who realised that collection wasn't just a head position.

Many horse owners realised there was a different way (to what was traditional or fashionable to their local area) to work with a horse, a way that combined performance and partnership together.

I got emails from people who were going to sell their horse, but instead tried out some of the methods in the documentary and had since built amazing partnerships together.

Horse owners told me that they were inspired to replace harsh bits with bitless options.

I am still getting emails and messages from people who watched the documentary. It has really taken me by surprise to hear how big an impact this documentary has had on so many horse people.

As I was making the documentary, I thought if I could change the world for just one horse, it would be worth it. But the reaction to it surpassed even my wildest expectations. It showed me that there is an incredible community of horse owners in the world who firmly believe in the importance of listening to the horse.

Homework:

Grab a bag of popcorn and get a free ticket to watch episode 1 of Listening to the Horse at: www.listentothehorse.com

The Principles of Listening to the Horse

After my travels, my studies, working with my horses, creating the documentary and hearing from so many fantastic people around the world who were committed to doing the best for their horses - I had to find a way to share the approach that I believe is the best and fairest way to be with horses.

So I've produced films, online courses, workshops, podcasts and everything I could think of to communicate with like-minded people. I want to share the principles which are the foundations of Listening to the Horse:

1. Our greatest judge is our horse. So we put our horse's physical and mental health first, regardless of what anyone else might say.
2. We take as long as it takes and we appreciate the power of time and patience.
3. We aim to be open minded, curious, consistent, patient and kind.
4. We understand improving our horsemanship is a lifelong journey.
5. We recognise the try, no matter how slight.
6. We don't use shortcuts, quick fixes, gadgets, draw reins, tie our horses heads down or tie their mouths shut.
7. We do not place competition goals above our horse's health.
8. We don't pull on our horses.
9. We don't support riding horses in hyperflexion or the practise of Rollkur.
10. We understand collection is not a head position.

11. We understand that for collection to happen there needs to be a shift of weight from the forequarters to the hindquarters.
12. We know that self-carriage means that the horse does it by himself.
13. We believe that groundwork builds relaxation, partnership and connection.
14. We are proud to walk on foot with our horses and we know that every mile counts.
15. We know that true horsemanship begins with relaxation and confidence.
16. We understand the importance of riding and training our horses in a way that will improve their long term physical health.
17. We believe true horsemanship is an art form that develops softness, lightness and true connection, and we follow the traditions that honour this.
18. We live in the present and stay emotionally neutral, with an open mind and a desire to understand.
19. We allow our horses time to evolve at their own pace.
20. We appreciate there are often differences between what the rider wants and what the horse needs.
21. We accept the fact that the horse has more to teach us than we will ever teach them.
22. We acknowledge that a horse's body is only physically mature at a minimum of 5.5 years of age, and the back is the last part to develop. So we don't ride 2 or 3 years olds.
23. We understand that older horses are not disposable and it's our duty to care for them in their last years.
24. We are aware that developing a horse correctly through balance, timing and feel takes years.
25. We don't typecast or stereotype horses according to sex, age, colour or breed. We work with the horse in front of us and leave pre-conceptions by the door.
26. We are prepared to quieten our minds in order to hear our horses, however softly they are speaking.
27. We understand horsemanship is a never-ending journey and we always must put the horse first.

28. We support each other on our individual journeys and value the friendships we create along the way.

Cornerstones

Having a series of exercises and lessons to reach certain goals with your horse can be very useful. However your success doesn't solely depend on how many exercises you know, or how often you do them.

Your success will also directly depend on your approach, your attitude and the philosophy you use while you are with your horse. There are 11 cornerstones that are the foundations of the Listening to the Horse approach.

1. Eat the elephant
2. Learning to help
3. Power of consistency
4. Comfort zones
5. Delayed gratification
6. The try and the reward
7. Unlabel your horse
8. Horse health
9. Avoid gadgets
10. Age and goals
11. The rollercoaster

Eat the elephant

There is a wonderful line in the Listening to the Horse documentary, and it goes like this: "Ask very little, and reward generously." I love this philosophy and I try to use it whenever I can. However it can create its own problems. Many horse owners have dreams they want to achieve with their horses. Asking very little might be great in theory, but what if you want to do something BIG with your horse? What if you have a BIG goal you want to achieve?

- Like having a relaxing trail ride with your horse.
- Or enjoying a day riding with your friends on the beach.
- Or your horse being happy to walk into a horse trailer.
- Or doing your first shoulder in and out.

Don't we need to ask our horse to do big things as well as small things?

The answer is 'yes and no'. There is an old joke that you may have heard…

"How do you eat an elephant?
One bite at a time."

Anything we need to do with our horses, be it big or small, I believe can be broken down into lots of tiny parts. Then we do each tiny part on its own and give our horses a lot of praise for each tiny part we accomplish. That way you can achieve your goals, and all your mini-goals along the way, PLUS make it super easy for your horse to understand first these small stages then the bigger things.

The key to success for this approach is strategic planning.

Ozzie and the pole of death

When I bought Ozzie as a five year old Connemara at the sales in Kilkenny, Ireland, it was very important to me that he was relaxed and confident in all situations. During the first few days in his new home I discovered he had very little confidence. In fact, most things worried him a lot.

One issue Ozzie had was with poles on the ground, or any type of jump. In Ireland young horses get asked to trot and canter, without a rider, over jumps. The concept is if you are selling a young horse the prospective buyers will want to see if your horse has jumping ability. So horses get lunged in a halter and on a long rope - and often get scared - during this training process. This probably happened to Ozzie.

When I asked Ozzie to walk beside me, and walk over a pole on the ground, he was fine. But when I asked him, during groundwork, to just trot slowly over a pole on the ground he would bolt over it.

Every single time.

He would literally take off at speed, I couldn't stop him. Then when he stopped, his breathing would be heavy, his body tense and his eyes carried a lot of worry and fear. This 'bolt over a pole' pattern was one unfortunate thing the previous owners had taught him. It wasn't going to work for me. I did not want Ozzie deciding he had to bolt every time he saw a pole on the ground! So I needed to fix it. I had a big goal.

My next step was to write down a list of mini-goals that would lead me to my big goal.

When you are creating a list of mini-goals for your horse, there are 2 factors to consider:

- You will need to be prepared to get really creative.
- Your #1 goal should be to change how the horse feels about the situation. When you can change how the horse feels, then the horse will change it's behaviour.

Ozzie's bolting over the poles wasn't a physical issue. Ozzie's problem was because he remembered what had happened in the past when he went over poles at a trot and canter. His memory of that experience made him feel afraid and unconfident. If I could help Ozzie feel relaxed and happy going over poles, the bolting would stop.

My first mini-step was for Ozzie to walk over the pole and feel relaxed. This he could do already, so it was a great easy step 1.

The next mini step was to trot over the pole with *less* panicking. No panicking would be too big a goal at this stage! This was a tricky one to fix. At the slightest hint of a super slow trot, Ozzie would take off so fast I couldn't stop him. I didn't want to try to fix this by pulling on the lead rope, or letting him "hit" the end of it as this creates different problems in the future. So I needed a different approach.

The current situation was that Ozzie would bolt over the pole then panic and stop himself after 4-5 steps on the other side. So I had to think for a while to figure out the next mini step. One option might have been to see if I could use a fence line or anything in my environment in a creative way, to make the bolting a little more tricky. As we were in a paddock with wire fencing that wouldn't work. Instead, I decided on a different approach.

I decided Ozzie and I would walk over the pole on the ground, which he was happy to do. Then I would ask Ozzie to do the slowest trot in history over the pole. Regardless of how fast he went, once he stopped by himself I would tell him he was wonderful, and the session would be over.

I figured one of the best ways I could help him understand he would never have to worry about poles again, would be to offer him HUGE rewards when he went over the pole. There would be a lot of kind words, a rest and then we would finish the session. The plan would be to use time to my advantage as a reward, and each pole session would be no more than three minutes long. Then I would take off the halter and he would be free to eat and relax in the paddock. I knew three minute sessions were probably something he was not used to!

So this is what we did. For the first couple of sessions, nothing really changed. Oz would walk over the pole fine. Then when I asked him to trot, as soon as he came near the pole he would bolt, then stop in a panic on the other side. I would tell him he was great, and we would finish. He'd look at me as if to say - "That was it, Elaine? Really?"

After a few days, something odd happened. Ozzie would still panic when I asked him to trot slowly over a pole. But the panic started to become less. I continued to ask him, and I accepted what he did -

whatever it was. Then I ended the session, and told him he was wonderful.

As the days went on - and we probably did 10-14 days like this - the bolting started to look more like a fast trot. Then the fast trot started to look more like an energetic trot. Until one day, a good two weeks later, Ozzie did his first slow trot on a loose rein over the pole on the ground.

Just like the pole wasn't even there. Just like there had never been an issue. I was so proud of him.

Ozzie and I ate the elephant. By breaking down one difficult task into a lot of smaller, more bite-sized chunks. We also allowed ourselves a lot of time to fix it, in fact, as much time as we needed. We spent two slow weeks on this, but got it fixed perfectly.

It wasn't what I personally wanted to be doing (I still had my dreams of cantering across the fields!) but I had to start where my horse was (scared of poles!) and begin our training there.

The problem Ozzie had with the poles was a two-week problem. That was how long it took to build his confidence and fix this issue properly. The time it takes to fix any issue is dictated solely by the horse. However the good news is with each issue you fix the greater the connection and partnership you build together. So 'eating the elephant', and breaking down each goal you have into a large number of tiny tasks is a great way to work with your horse.

Homework:

Pick 1 horse related goal you want to achieve and write down at least 10 mini steps/goals to get there.

Learning to help

One approach that is not very useful with horses, is the *'show him who is boss and make 'em do it'* approach. The fact is that a horse is not just a physical object to be made to move to specific places when wanted. For example past a scary rock on a trail ride, or into a horse trailer. They are living, thinking beings who deserve to be allowed some time. In fact, horses are very smart. If we can use the approach of 'helping' the horse, rather than 'making' the horse do things, life becomes a lot easier and safer too.

The scary gap

It was a beautiful sunny day in Ireland and I was riding Ozzie in the field at home. We were alone and approaching a muddy gap, which looked a bit scary to Ozzie. As we were walking about 15 metres away from the muddy gap Ozzie slowed down and started to get worried. I noticed his breathing had changed, and tension had started to develop in his body. What should I do next?

The most common approach usually follows the *'make 'em do it'* philosophy. The rider would start to use the legs to put on pressure, to ask the horse to keep moving forwards. The horse would get a little more worried, get more tense, and start moving backwards or sideways - trying to get further away from the scary gap. The rider in return would apply more pressure... and the situation would go downhill from there.

Even if the rider managed to get the horse past the scary location, the horse's confidence level, and their trust in their rider - who had just ignored how they felt - would have deteriorated.

Instead, I like to think that whatever I do today my goal is to help my horse be 1% better tomorrow. Then maybe 1% better the day after that, until one day there is no longer an issue. So if my horse is scared of a muddy gap that he is unsure about, how do I help him increase his confidence level so that one day it will no longer be a problem for him?

Instead of putting on more leg pressure, I went the other direction. When Ozzie slowed down and stopped, at a distance away from the gap that Ozzie deemed acceptable, that was fine by me. We stood there quietly, listening to the birds play on the pond nearby, and with Ozzie keeping an unsure eye on the scary gap. We stood there calmly for about a minute, regarding the scary gap at this safe distance.

Each issue has a time associated with fixing it properly. This may be five minutes, two weeks, 12 months or longer. At the beginning it can be difficult to figure this out, so I was curious to see how much time it would take for Ozzie to work through this. I was in no rush. When I was sitting in the saddle I felt completely relaxed. Because we were still at a distance from the scary gap that Ozzie was happy with there was no risk of spooking, bolting for danger.

Instead I used one of the oldest tricks in the book to help my horse - I did nothing and gave him time to think about it. About two minutes later, Ozzie decided to take one step a little forwards and then one step to the side. Then he stood in this new spot and again stared intently at the scary gap. When approaching something they are unsure of horses like to be able to check it out from different angles. At this stage, I was just a passenger in the saddle. I was just sitting there with a loose rein, giving Ozzie time to think and figure it out. I never asked him to go forward. I never applied any pressure with my voice or legs. Instead I told him he was being very brave and rubbed his neck. But I never asked him to step forward towards the gap.

Horses are really curious, after another minute or two Ozzie decided he could take a few steps closer! So he carefully walked a little way forward. He was about three metres away from the scary gap now. He reached out his neck to sniff the scary gap area. After another minute, he decided to both carefully and slowly walk through the scary gap.

Ozzie made the decision once his feeling of fear had been replaced with a feeling of curiosity.
At no point had I put any force or pressure on him to do that.

If Ozzie had decided he didn't want to go through the scary gap that would have been fine with me. I had two other great options I could have tried at that stage:

1. Use the eat the elephant approach, go home, break it down into lots of smaller steps and work on it over the next 3-7-14 days - or whatever time it took.
2. Dismount and walk through it myself with Ozzie.

If you are riding and find yourself in a situation where you would feel more comfortable on the ground, or you could help your horse better on the ground, I would always recommend dismounting. It's about doing what is best for the horse to build confidence, and doing what will keep you both safe. There is no failure in doing what is best for your horse. It is a lot better than pressuring your horse, potentially falling off your horse or losing your horse's trust by overwhelming them. I have great admiration for someone who dismounts to fix a problem, or to stay safe and not lose their confidence or that of their horse. It shows true horsemanship and consideration for themselves and the horse.

The funniest thing was what happened after he decided to walk through the scary gap. Ozzie was so proud of himself! He felt so confident and happy. His ears were pricked forwards and he was marching through the next field like he owned it. I was so proud of him too. We had a lovely time exploring together and both of us felt super confident. It was a lovely afternoon.

When Ozzie and I eventually returned home, I realised I had forgotten to close the gate that was up at the scary gap. So I turned Ozzie around and we rode back up there. This time there was no hesitation on Ozzie's part.

- Ozzie saw the scary gap.
- He marched beautifully right up to it.
- Without any issues or change in speed or relaxation, Ozzie walked proudly straight through it!

I felt so proud of my horse.

Being aware there was going to be a situation (which was possible as I was paying attention, and not talking to a friend or taking photos on my phone!), acknowledging how my horse felt in the situation, and then allowing him to spend time in a safe area (at a distance from the scary object) allowed Ozzie to change how he felt.

A lot more can be achieved with horses when we ask ourselves 'how can we help our horse?' instead of 'how can we make our horse?'.

By using compassion for Ozzie's worry, and patience to allow him the time to figure it out - instead of forcing him through the scary gap and losing confidence - I was able to increase levels of trust, connection and partnership between myself and Ozzie.

Homework:

Write down 1 task or challenge you want to improve with your horse. Write down what you could do to 'make the horse do it'. Write down 3 different ways you could 'help the horse' to do it.

Tip: You can help your horse to be confident by trying out more things first on the ground. Another way to improve your horse's overall confidence levels is to work on the same thing in different locations.

The power of consistency

I met Matilda, a five year old Irish sports horse mare, for the first time at the spring horse sales in Goresbridge, Kilkenny about three years ago.

I had been looking for a young horse and she fit the bill perfectly. She was about 15.2 hands high, was un-ridden and had done very little. She had nice confirmation and moved very well. She seemed confident and relaxed too, which was also very important to me.

I had been through years of major confidence issues with Ozzie my Connemara, so I was hoping my new horse wouldn't have had any bad experiences in the past.

After a little negotiation, Matilda had a new human (me!) and we loaded her into the horsebox and set off for home.

Now, when you're driving home with a new horse in the horsebox behind you, you do hope that she will get along with your other horses. There are definitely situations where horses can 100% not get along - to the point that it's not safe for them to be together in a paddock. The plan was to put Matilda in her own paddock, which would be right beside Ozzie's paddock.

So we arrived home and everyone was very excited. My horses Ozzie and Dougal were very captivated as a new lovely lady had magically appeared! Matilda wasn't as impressed. Understandably, she had no idea where she was, who we were, or what she was doing here!

Everyone seemed to co-exist for a few days in their respective paddocks. Then one morning when I came out to feed them, the wire between Ozzie and Matilda's paddock had been trashed, and Ozzie and Matilda were in the same paddock, but on either side of it!

I watched them for a little while, and here is what was happening. Matilda had no interest in Ozzie whatsoever. Ozzie had put one of his Connemara plans in motion. He was first pretending to ignore Matilda. Then, in a very relaxed way, he slowly approached her while he also pretended he was just eating grass. Then he ended up standing right behind her - and then he bit her tail hard!

Whenever Ozzie did this Matilda would squeal and Ozzie would turn and gallop off as fast as his legs would carry him, before she had a chance to double-barrel him with her hind legs. They really didn't get on! Eventually, once they started to tolerate each other, it was time to move them officially to the same paddock. Matilda made sure Ozzie knew that she was the boss.

Now each morning everyone gets a small bucket of food. When Matilda was still pretty new here, when I went out to feed them in the paddock, I would put the two buckets down on the ground. Ozzie and Matilda started to eat their breakfast.

Matilda eats at the speed of light. So she had her bowl licked clean in about 30 seconds. Ozzie eats more slowly and savours every bite. Matilda immediately realised once she finished, that Ozzie still had food, and so marched over to push him off his bucket, so she could eat it.

"No so fast girly!" I thought.

I stepped in, made a bit of noise and flapped my arms to push her away. Well - she was not impressed at all! We got head-shaking, aerial acrobatics, a bit of galloping around and a horse who could NOT understand why she couldn't eat all of Ozzie's breakfast! She displayed a lot of dramatics!! Anyway, we got over that and she stayed away. Ozzie finished his breakfast and that was it.

Every morning since then, the two horses are in the same paddock, and they each get their bucket. After the first few days of displeasure when I had to stop Matilda from eating Ozzie's food, she resigned herself to the situation. Every day the same thing happened:

- *Elaine, I finished my breakfast. It was delicious!*
- *That's great Matilda.*
- *Elaine, I really need to eat Ozzie's breakfast now.*
- *No you don't, Matilda.*
- *Bother! OK. I'll go eat some grass then I guess.*
- *Sounds good, Matilda.*

Every day she asks the same question. Every day she gets the same answer.

These days instead of her throwing a big wobbly when I say no, she asks me the question (at this stage I can see the thought forming in her mind!) I just quietly say 'no' under my breath, and she turns away from Ozzie and looks for some grass instead.

No drama.

No confusion.

No problem.

One of the most important lessons we learn, as people who strive to listen to the horse, is to be 100% clear in our actions, and to be 110% consistent in our answers. Every day - with one word said quietly - I communicate clearly with Matilda about something that is very important to her. If SOME days - I allowed her to eat Ozzie's food - it would be a NIGHTMARE!! She has a lot of energy and determination - and would have used that to get the food if I wasn't crystal clear - every single day.

Consistency changes everything when you are working with a horse. From enjoyable calm meal times, to connected groundwork and on to developing that true connection, lightness and softness in your riding.

Homework:

Choose 3 small things you are going to be completely consistent about this year with your horse.

Comfort zones

There is a very useful concept that I learned from Steve Halfpenny that I'd like to share with you. It makes working with any horse so much easier. It will hugely increase your confidence and your horse's confidence too. It is the concept of using three different comfort zones with your horse.

At the most simple level, your horse's comfort zone is most often directly related to their physical location and geographical areas.

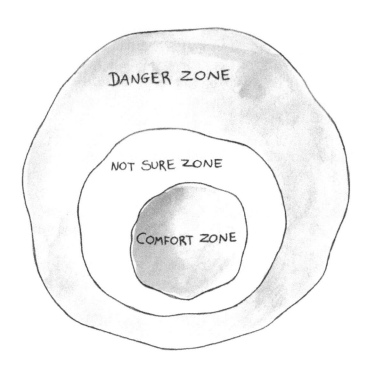

- The Comfort Zone - If your horse is somewhere they feel safe, they will generally be relaxed and happy. The first zone is the 'comfort zone', which will be any area where your horse feels safe and relaxed. Usually this will be around their barn, stables, and paddocks - in other words the areas where they are probably near other horses. When a horse is in his comfort zone he will find it easy to focus on you. He will find it easy to learn new things. As he is relaxed and confident, the human will also tend to feel relaxed and confident in these locations.

- The Not So Sure Zone - The next zone is the 'not sure zone'. These will likely be just a bit further out than the 'comfort zone', but you might also find them elsewhere. When your horse is in a not sure zone they will not feel quite so confident or relaxed. Instead they can feel anxious or nervous. Their breathing may have got faster. They will be starting to ignore you a little and instead be focused on, or listening to, something that is distracting or starting to trouble them. They haven't panicked yet - but there's definitely a lot more anxiety going on. Often because the horse's level of worry and tension has increased, the human's will increase also.

- The Danger Zone - The third zone is the 'danger zone'. The danger zone is any area where the horse is really worried and can't listen to their human at all. When they are in this state they pretty much think they're going to die. For them it is a life or death situation. In this zone horses can react by running you over, bolting, spooking or displaying other sudden movements. They are telling us that they have an extreme lack of both confidence and relaxation. It is incredibly difficult to teach a horse anything useful when they are in the danger zone. It can also be very unsafe for the human when the horse is in this situation. So ideally we want to avoid putting our horses in the danger zone.

The first step is to figure out where your horse's three zones are. They will be different for each horse. They can also change daily!

Homework:

I would like you to get a pen and paper and draw a map of where your horse lives. Include all stables, paddocks, laneways, roads, fields and trails around the property.

- I would like you to colour in everywhere your horse is confident and relaxed in a green highlighter. These areas are all part of your horse's comfort zone. It is fine to teach your horse new things here, as you will have the greatest chance of success.
- I would like you to colour everywhere on the map where your horse is 'not sure' in an orange highlighter. These not sure areas will be places you can visit briefly, but I would recommend spending most of your time in the comfort zone areas.
- Lastly, please colour any danger zones in red. As there are huge safety concerns here I would avoid these areas for the time being.

You might be reading these and feel demoralised because your horse has a very small comfort zone right now. But there is a magic secret about comfort zones.

Comfort zones change over time. The more time you spend with your horse in their comfort zone, the larger that comfort zone will grow.

To apply the zones, start by making sure that you work with your horse mainly in their comfort zone. Spend a little bit of time in the not so sure zone - maybe 5% - 10% of your time together - but always return to their comfort zone to reassure them and let them relax and think. Stay away from the danger zones, and if you inadvertently find yourself in them, move into a safer area as quickly as possible.

As you work in this way, over days or maybe weeks (it depends on your horse) the comfort zone will gradually expand into the not so sure zone. You will suddenly realise that parts of the danger zone have become not so sure zones. Re-draw your map and colour it in, maybe every 4-6 weeks. It will show you that you and your horse are becoming braver and more confident together!

The biggest indicator of success is to be aware of where exactly your horse's comfort zones are each day and to adjust your plan accordingly.

"I bought a warmblood mare a couple months ago. She was pretty green, especially given she was already 12, but she walked, trotted, and cantered under saddle for me in a relatively relaxed and balanced way when I tried her and I was looking for a project. When I brought her home I discovered several issues that were not disclosed by the previous owner including that she was heartbreakingly unconfident in new situations and horribly herd bound as a result. Frankly she was dangerous when she was upset - threatening to run her handler over on the ground and rear under saddle. Her favorite trick when she didn't want to do something was to go flying backwards in an attempt to get away. She actually fell over and scraped up her hind legs more than once doing this.

Naturally I realized I was not going to be riding any time soon. I spent a month reaffirming her ground work and she got much better staying out of my space, yielding her shoulder, disengaging her haunch, halting, backing, and changing direction with soft cues but she never stopped being busy. It was like her feet couldn't rest any more than her mind and I was always struggling to keep her attention on me. She'd whinny for her mares constantly and look around even as I gave her commands.

Then my mom suggested Elaine Heney's free 5 Day Horse Confidence Workshop that mom was participating in with her young thoroughbred. One of the days, Elaine discussed comfort zones and a lightbulb went off. I decided to work my mare in her field with her mares in their feed pens eating hay to see what would happen. It was a miracle! She actually stood still for minutes at a time! Her head was down and the tension gone from her body; she looked more like a quarter horse than a hot warmblood.

I immediately purchased the TrailBrave program. We're only on day 7 but today Elle left her pen and walked around the neighboring field and the retention pond (with its duck) all while her buddy screamed for her. She raised her head a couple times and whinnied once but never took a single trot step, and she stood still in both areas for several minutes at a time without crowding my space.

I wish I had videos of when she first came home because it's hard to make people understand just how big of an accomplishment standing still is for this mare. Already she is so much calmer and more confident. She no longer needs to search for other horses to feel safe, and I can't wait to see how she grows as I continue with the program. I never imagined something as simple as a safe zone would make such a difference. I can't express my gratitude enough."
Kristin, USA.

Delayed gratification

We live in a world where so many things have become instant. It's much easier for humans to focus on short term goals which have immediate rewards, rather than choosing long term goals.

It's nice to get a takeaway dinner delivered in 30 minutes and not have to cook! Or ordering something in five minutes for next day delivery on Amazon without leaving home - instead of putting on your jacket, putting petrol in your car, driving to town & spending two hours walking around to see if you can find what you need.

With horses fixing problems and working on improving ourselves can take some effort, especially at the beginning of the journey. So you can feel sometimes like you're making very little progress. But in fact you are working on the most critical lessons for your horse, which are all of the foundations you will need in place for later on down the road.

So we need patience when things take longer than expected. But the good news is that taking time in the early stages to get to know your horse & build trust & communication, will pay off in dividends over your years together.

By spending the time putting in all the foundations, we will achieve much higher goals with our horses in the future, than if we skipped these important lessons.

"I bought my Welsh cob Leo six months ago. He is 9 years old and was sold as a ridden horse. When I got him back to the stables it was quickly apparent that he was far from that. After a few days

settling I tacked him up in order to try out a new saddle and I needed to mount, that's where the problems became apparent.

He refused to let me mount, spun round, backed up and appeared terrified of anyone on his back; despite me having ridden him prior to purchasing. I was beside myself and a friend who was with me at the time said I should send him back. He had come from a hunting yard where he had not been interacted with much apart from 'breaking' and turning away so I felt he had never had the attention he deserved, he was essentially quite feral and clearly he didn't trust people at all.

After a lot of tears, anxiety, soul searching and stress I decided that sending him back was not an option and although he was not what I expected I would learn how to deal with this and work things out. I decided to concentrate on gaining his trust, allowing him to build confidence in me and himself. Now 6 months down the line I still haven't ridden him properly but we have a bond and I don't feel the need to rush him into it. We walk for miles, play, do groundwork, pole work and generally hang around together. He follows me in the field and is a different horse to the nervous crazed animal who arrived at the yard, he's actually quite cheeky now and his personality really shines through.

We still have our issues to work through but I've found letting go of the initial expectations and owning what we are doing has taught me to be less impatient in lots of other aspects of life (and I am notoriously impatient)! He's taught me a lot in that respect and although others may judge and mock me because I have yet to ride my horse, I know that when I do he will be confident in me and our connection will keep us both safe. Then watch us fly!" Chantelle, UK.

Buying a new horse in Kilkenny

When I bought Ozzie, he was five years old and had allegedly just been started and ridden for eight weeks before the sales. I brought him home and it soon became evident that it would have been a lot easier to work with Ozzie, if no one had ever done anything with him!

Firstly I couldn't touch him or catch him. He was afraid of everything. Halters, numnahs/saddle pads, saddles, girths. The noise that a girth made. He was scared in most areas. Birds in bushes resulted in massive spooks. A quad bike approaching resulted in a 180 spin and bolt.

I remember working with Ozzie - mostly on the ground - for the first few years. It was so tough. At times it required a PhD in patience. Every horse is different, and one important lesson Ozzie taught me was the minefield system.

A minefield is a large area with a significant number of mines waiting to blow up if you stumble over them. Imagine you need to find and defuse them. With horses I'd compare this to the number of issues you need to resolve.

When you step out onto the minefield, you discover your first issue (or the first mine) that you need to fix. You use the elephant method and a lot of patience, and very slowly you work to build confidence and fix that issue. Issue #1 took a lot of work to fix, but you're very happy now it's all sorted.

Then you look up and take your next step into the mindfield. You discover 3 more mines. Your heart sinks. You commit to working through them and defusing them one by one, and six weeks later, all three issues are now resolved. You feel great!

Then you look up and take the next step into a minefield. There are four new issues. All of them also need to be fixed. You put your head in your hands and despair. You are sure that at some stage someone told you that owning a horse was meant to be fun! This isn't turning out to be fun at all! Instead it is just one long list of problems that need to be fixed. You have no idea exactly how many of those problems are even on the list. It can be very demoralising and incredibly difficult to keep going.

It seemed like a long road to travel, but once in a while I would get a tiny glimpse of something magical with Ozzie. A moment of feeling connected, of feeling like we were slowly building a partnership together - despite all the challenges. A moment of hope.

I knew that to achieve my goal to have a happy, confident and amazing riding horse I needed to put in years of effort to work on all of the foundations and fix the long list of baggage that Ozzie had arrived with.

Honestly, there were times when I didn't know if I would ever get to the end of 'fixing' things. Helping a horse is the opposite of instant gratification, but as horse owners, when we buy a horse, that's what we sign up to.

After a few years suddenly, one day, I noticed that the problems Ozzie had arrived with had gone. Instead of my 'to do' list being full of issues I had to fix, I had a new to do list. Finally it included some stuff that was actually fun!

- Like going out on a trail ride, without any drama.
- Like doing my first shoulder out on the ground, without a fence line.

- Like doing my first ridden walk pirouette with no weight in my hands.

I had spent so many years working on confidence building, partnership and trust that once it was all fixed - I had ended up with an amazing riding horse.

One day, a few friends were visiting for a clinic. In the past, anytime I had offered a friend the opportunity to ride Ozzie for a few minutes, the answer had always been 'no thanks'. They had all seen the difficult times! At this clinic, Sophie, one of my friends, was riding her horse and working on softness and lightness. Once you ride a horse that can truly offer the rider softness and lightness, it is the most magical feeling in the world. Very few riders get to experience this. It's also very difficult to describe in words how this feels.

My friend was riding her lovely coloured horse. Steve Halfpenny, who was teaching at the clinic and working with Sophie, looked over at me and asked if it would be ok for Sophie to have a short ride on Ozzie, so she could feel how soft and light he was. I was completely honored and said "Sure, no problem."

I walked Ozzie over to Sophie, dismounted, held Sophie's horse Degri, and Sophie brought Ozzie over to the mounting block and got on. This is what happened, in Sophie's words.

"I was working on Degri's lightness - a quicker response when I applied my aids. I also wanted to make sure the aids were not heavily applied, meaning no muscular effort needed on my part. I wanted to use just a touch.

When I got on Ozzie, he reacted straight away with my aids, especially with his hindquarters. My leg barely touched his side a little behind the saddle, and his hindquarters were at the ready! It felt very floating, like a gliding feeling. Asking him to step back was very subtle too, Just a shift in my body weight was needed.

Ozzie taught me two main things. He taught me that light use of the aids is a reality. He embodied the saying 'less is more'. But he also taught me to be very aware of what you are asking. I felt that I confused him sometimes because I would not think of my leg, and I would allow it to tap his side and I could feel him moving his hind but not being sure. So this made me think of being more careful with my body. And that causes me to think more about focusing on my intention when using my aids also.

It was very useful to ride Ozzie, so I could get the feel, so I could try and get the same feeling with my own horse Degri. And it just shows it is possible to obtain such responses from a horse ridden bitless. It proved that it is not the gear or even the aids. It is the way they are applied and used. Thanks for the lesson, Ozzie!"

Offering our horses patience is not always easy, but it's something that they desperately need. It makes a huge positive impact in our horse training. Just like Ozzie, when you work on the foundations using as much patience as you can gather, the results can be remarkable.

Homework:

Rate your patience levels with your horse out of 10.

Try & reward

When I was growing up in Ireland I used to play a game called hot and cold. You have a group of people together. One person is the hunter. The other players decide on a mystery challenge for the hunter to complete.

- The challenge for the hunter might be to sit down on a certain chair.
- Or to touch their head with their right hand.
- Or to take a cup off the table.

The hunter has no idea what the challenge is. So the hunter must begin by trying random things. When the hunter is one step closer to completing the mystery challenge, maybe they've walked towards that table with the cup on it, the crowd says 'hotter'. When they take a step away from completing the mystery challenge, the crowd says 'colder'. So it's a fun game to play and we used to enjoy it a lot.

When we train our horses we can use a similar principle very effectively. Just like the hunter, the horse has no idea what we want them to learn.

- It could be to lower their head to put a halter on.
- To not be afraid when a colourful umbrella appears.
- Or maybe to do their first step backwards with a loose lead rope.

So we can use a similar strategy to help the horse figure it out.

It's called recognising the try. When the horse moves a tiny bit closer to the mystery challenge we call this a 'try'. When our horse gives us a 'try', just like in the hot and cold game, they need to know they are on the right path. So we give them what is known as a release.

The simplest release is when we give the horse peace. So if we are asking the horse to do something we stop asking and give them a rest instead.

Sometimes the horse can even give himself a release! This happens when they find a place of peace. It's an opportunity that is very valuable to offer especially when creating softness and lightness as we move to more advanced work with our horses. To begin, the easiest strategy to understand would be to give your horse a rest and a kind word any time you recognise a try.

I use this so much with my horses Ozzie and Matilda. The horses love it! They start doing huge yawns, they relax even more (which is wonderful) and I tell them they are the smartest horses in Ireland.

In fact, it was this exact strategy, along with a ton of patience, that changed Ozzie from a horse with a million issues to an incredible riding horse.

The key to using the try and the reward strategy is to make sure we can see what is going on. To be able to see when our horses are trying, when they are getting 'hotter' like in the hot and cold game, we really need to be paying a lot of attention to them. That means that when you are with your horse you must concentrate on them. You're not on Facebook, you're not talking to your friends, you're not thinking about the nasty person at work and you're not chatting on the phone. Your horse needs and deserves your full attention when you are with them.

Finally, in order to truly unlock the power of this approach, it's necessary to go one step further. A try can also be defined as that moment when your horse is thinking what you're thinking. Perhaps you are thinking that you would love your horse to take one step backwards. Then for a split second you feel your horse's body soften and there is the tiniest shift backwards in balance. Your horse has not yet moved a foot, but they are thinking of going backwards. That is the perfect place to give them a rest and reward the try.

I was at a small clinic where my friend was riding her Arab. For at least 3 years of clinics I'd watched these two struggle to get a true 'soft feel', not helped by the fact that the horse clearly had some issues in his neck. (Soft feel is that feeling when the horse is supple in the neck, their balance is on their hindquarters, and for the rider there is no weight in the reins.) So everyone had just started riding when my friend halted her horse, jumped off and left the arena. "What's wrong??" everyone asked. "Nothing" was the reply "I asked him to soften, felt him flex his poll and think back for a second, and ending the session is the biggest reward I can think of."

Over the next few days they carried on with the work. Every time my friend felt her horse get softer in the neck and give the tiniest change in balance there she was - out of the saddle! As things progressed she started to take him out of the arena to eat some grass, then return. Then over the next few days I could see that the horse 'got it' - he was starting to realise how much better he felt when he softened and was in balance and looking for it himself. After maybe 5 days they could walk a circle with the horse in a soft feel and offering self carriage.

Homework:

Choose 1 activity to use the hot and cold game with.

Unlabel your horse

In our Facebook online community I have one rule that some might think is weird. No one is allowed to write up a post which calls their horse any type of negative word - like..

"My horse is stupid."
"My horse is a brat."
Etc…

I understand why people might do this. Horses are not easy. Some situations we find ourselves in with horses can cause us a lot of frustration. One way to try and let go and release some of that frustration is to blame the horse and call it some type of negative word. However, when we do that, what we are doing is blaming the horse. Then the next time we see the horse we enter into the moment in a bad frame of mind. If we think our horse is a 'brat', then we will automatically change the way we treat them. We are going to be less patient. We may be more physical or louder in our actions. We are going to do all the things that are likely to cause the horse to lose more confidence and actually make the situation worse.

Good horsemanship demands that we never lose our tempers or our patience with our horses.

The sad thing about this situation is that quite often any unwanted behaviour from the horse that makes us frustrated may actually be because the horse is in pain.

- Bites you when you tighten the girth? He may have ulcers.
- Won't stand still at the mounting block? The saddle might be pinching his back.
- Keeps opening his mouth and tossing his head in the air when you ride? The metal bit might be banging off a tooth or not be a good fit for his mouth.

So we need to unlabel the horse.

Because it's never the horse's fault. Even in the cases when it is not pain related, we cannot blame the horse. They are simply trying to survive each moment the best way they can. I call it 'horses being horses'.

When you are working with a horse who is struggling, there is one mindset change that has helped me to avoid frustration. I change my mindset from blaming the horse, to feeling sorry because the horse is going through a difficult situation. When I switch to feeling empathy for the horse, then it's much easier for me to focus on how I can best help the horse - whatever the situation may be.

- It could be me deciding that I won't jump to conclusions, and instead I'll double check everything I can to see if there could be any causes of pain anywhere on the horse's body.
- It could be arranging a checkup from the vet, dentist or physiotherapist.
- It could be me realising that I am tired and worn out and my frustration has nothing to do with the horse.
- It could be me realising that putting blame on the horse will only get me further away from my goals with my horse.
- It could be me realising that I need to slow down and change my expectations. I am trying to teach my horse advanced algebra when they are still figuring out basic addition - so of course it's ever going to work well!

"I can't stand to hear people calling their horses bad names. Horses learn or do not learn from us, the owner. No one to blame but ourselves." Barbara, USA.

Homework:

Commit to not referring to your horse with any type of negative names.

Horse's health

In Ireland there is a national training programme called the Green Cert. It's a full time six week course for young farmers. A few years ago I decided it was time to get my certification. I arrived at the class each day in my finest wellies along with about 40 other farmers. Over the six weeks we got lessons on everything from forestry to dairy farming!

Every now and again we used to go on a 'farm visit' and we would all take off on the back roads of Ireland looking for a specific dairy or tillage farm. These particular trips had a great air of excitement about them, as you never knew where you were going. We took off in a convoy of mud splattered cars and jeeps. The set-up was that only the first car knew the actual location of the farm. So it was critical that when driving you kept the car in front of you in sight. If you lost sight, you would spend the next three hours driving around lost looking for a random farm!

As part of the six weeks of training, as farming can be a very physical job, we had a few classes on health and safety and PPE (personal protective equipment) like using face masks, protective clothing, hard hats when needed etc. There was one class which I still remember. We were all in the classroom, and this guy comes out and proceeds to spend about 1 hour teaching me the correct way to lift something heavy. (The short version is to bend your knees and keep your back straight!). Not only had we to learn the exact method, but then we all had to go up to the top of the classroom and demonstrate it! All 40 of us individually! But it does make sense. Farmers are often lifting heavy objects, from hay bales and machinery parts to gates and fencing equipment and they can't afford to damage themselves.

If you lift any type of weight without being careful about how you lift it, it's unfortunately easy to damage your back. No one wants a sore back. I know some people with back issues which have really impacted their health.

- A cousin of mine had a slipped disc that was incredibly painful and lasted for quite a while and hugely affected her health.
- A equestrian friend of mine in Spain developed a back problem. This meant she wasn't able to ride horses for a few months. Eventually, it got so bad she had to go into hospital for a week to try and get it fixed.
- A friend of mine has a 'dodgy back', and every few months it flares up and they need to wear a brace to try and protect it.

Back problems are not good. So I was very happy to get the training during the green cert!

A few years later, I was working up in Sligo and my friend Sara was working in one of the many pharmaceutical companies up there. She was a health and safety officer. I was curious, so one day I asked her what she did in her job. Because pharmaceutical companies are so tightly regulated (which makes total sense) there were about a zillion processes, procedures and checkboxes that Sara had to make sure everyone was following correctly. Then she threw in a funny comment...

"Tomorrow, we are doing lifting training and assessment for the whole company."

"What?!" I said.

It turned out that there was a whole system about what an individual could lift, should never lift and how exactly to lift objects. It took me right back to my green cert training. It transpired that in both the agricultural and pharmaceutical industries in Ireland - and many more I would presume - doing everything you can do to protect the health of your back is critical. Oddly, it's exactly the same with horses.

If you think about it, we ask horses to carry a heavy weight - the rider - every time we ride. So just like we teach farmers and lab workers to adopt a specific posture when carrying a heavy object in order to protect their backs from strain, we need to do exactly the same with our horses. We know how important it is to do everything we can to avoid back pain and that goes for our horses too.

The situation is that when we sit on our horses we put all this extra weight on their backs. Depending on the size of the rider that's usually anywhere from 8 stones, or 50 kg, upwards. However, unlike the farming and pharmaceutical industries who teach all their employees how to protect their backs and carry weight with a safe posture, very few riders actually teach their horses this.

So many horses get back trouble later in life, which can be hugely painful. Some horses even have to retire at a young age (less than 10 years old) as they can no longer be ridden due to back issues - from kissing spines (a horrible diagnosis) to all sorts of damage to their muscles or to the ligaments that hold the vertebrae in alignment. It's a lot more common than we think. As part of being a responsible horse rider and owner it's critical that we include teaching our horses how to carry the rider's weight in the saddle, using good posture that will protect the horse's back. Just like my friend Sara taught her colleagues and my green cert trainer taught me.

The question is - what way should the horse carry a rider? And how on earth can we teach a horse to change his posture when a rider is on board? The answer is actually quite straightforward. The horse has four legs, two fore legs and two hind legs. If we can encourage the horse to carry a little less weight on his front two legs, and a little more weight on his hind two legs, this helps the horse to carry the rider's weight much more easily.

This is something that every rider who rides should make it their goal to do in the next 1-3 months. As horse owners we owe it to our horses to teach them everything we know to protect their long-term physical health, so that we can avoid causing them any pain when we ride.

The first two exercises I recommend to begin to influence the horse's posture are called shoulder out and shoulder in. I usually teach them to the horse first when walking beside them on the ground. Once the horse has learned them they can be repeated in the saddle. These two exercises ask the horse to take a deeper step with each hind leg, so the hind legs step deeper under the horse's body. When this happens the horse's centre of gravity changes. This results in the horse carrying a little more weight on their hindquarters, and a little less weight on their forequarters.

It might sound a little complicated, but I promise you the exercises are easy to do once you understand them, and any horse owner can do them. I'll share the exact steps I use to teach these exercises to my horse, and they are super simple! I promise you that you will be able to do them too.

Not only will you be having fun riding your horse, you'll also have the peace of mind to know that you are improving your horse's posture and long term health while you train. You will be drastically reducing the chances of back pain in your horse's future.

Homework:

Find two people you know who have back problems. Interview them and ask them how it has affected their daily life.

Avoiding gadgets

Gadgets are things that people use with horses when they:

- Have a goal they are finding difficult to solve.
- Have a goal they want to solve quickly.
- Have a lack of information about how to solve a goal without a gadget.
- Or maybe when the horse is displaying an unwanted behaviour, such as putting their head up in the air when ridden.

Examples of gadgets would include:

- The horse is opening its mouth when being ridden with a bit. So the owner buys a noseband that has an extra strap (known as a flash or a grackle) that will keep the horse's mouth closed. The issue there is that they have no idea what is causing their horse to open its mouth. It could be anything from a bit pinching the tongue and causing pain, to an ulcer on the inside of the horse's mouth. Both of which would be better addressed by a dentist visit and a bit review.

- The rider's goal is to have their horse bring its head down and keep its nose closer to his chest. This is a fashionable and unfortunate goal for some riders currently because they think it demonstrates an 'outline'. So the rider buys special reins that when attached to the horse's girth and bridle hold the horse's head down and tucked towards its chest. Fixing a horse's head like this is extremely damaging for the horse's posture and body.

There are many other examples.

If your horse is showing any type of unwanted behaviour using gadgets to minimise that unwanted behaviour is rarely a good idea for the horse.

If you have a performance goal you want to reach, but are struggling to get there, a gadget is not going to benefit you or your horse. Spending time improving your horsemanship education is usually a better option.

Putting a gadget on a horse to solve a perceived problem is like putting a plaster on a cut without first removing the piece of glass that is causing the pain and bleeding.

"I had a friend who had been struggling for a little while with her horse. Her horse had been inclined to throw her head up and down and riding was pretty stressful for both of them. The yard trainer fitted a martingale, which is a gadget that stops a horse throwing their head up too high. Then Kate watched a video of herself riding and wondered if maybe she was holding the reins rather tight, was she putting too much pressure on her horse's mouth? She took a leap of faith. She removed the martingale and took her horse to the arena. She rode around at a walk, letting her horse choose the direction, and concentrated on putting no pressure on the reins at all. At first her horse threw her head about a lot, almost enough to make her rider stop the experiment. Then, suddenly, the mare started to relax and the head tossing stopped. After a few minutes of relaxed riding Kate ended the session and put her back in the field.

This gave Kate some food for thought, and some increased confidence in herself. Maybe, just maybe, she could listen to the horse and help the two of them to a better ridden partnership. She stopped the lessons and quietly worked alone, concentrating on relying less on the reins and having lighter hands. It worked!" Karen, UK.

Homework:

Make a list of any gadgets you use that restrict the horse's natural movement. Eg. ties the horse's mouth closed, forces the horse's head into a specific position, etc.

Age and goals

It's said that the average human matures physically between 18 to 22 years old. At what age do you think your horse is physically mature? Some people look at a horse aged three and think "Wow, he's huge! This horse must be fully grown and ready for a saddle and bridle." In fact, the answer to that is a resounding no!

Regardless of the size of the horse or pony, or their breed, no horse or pony is fully physically mature until they are either 6 months before or after their 6th birthday. The last parts of the horse's body to mature are the growth plates found at the junction between the base of the neck and the withers. That is right in front of where the rider sits in the saddle. So if you start riding a horse before the body is physically mature you are running into a much greater risk of injury.

The sad thing about this is that in some parts of the world riding 2 and 3 year olds has become fashionable and accepted. Sometimes it is a necessary requirement because the goal is to enter certain competitions in order to win prizes and awards.

"Elaine's online community helped me decide to not saddle start my Appendix as a 2yo. His frame was too narrow & off balance, his mind too playful & without focus. I explained to my very Western, 2yo colt starter husband, that many English horses aren't started until 4yo & go on to professional careers, even the Olympics." Carlena, USA.

In order to compete in some reining competitions young horses are ridden and start training from 18-24 months old. The people who ride these youngsters are gambling with the health of the horse. For that reason I would never buy a young horse who has already had significant riding under the age of four. You simply don't know what long term negative impact that training will cause to the horse's health in the future.

You can definitely do various groundwork exercises that do not involve riding or carrying weight before the horse is fully mature. These can be very useful to help the horse build confidence, develop muscles and improve their postural habits before a rider gets onboard.

Both my horses, Ozzie and Matilda, were not ridden or backed until they were five years old. My horsemanship philosophy is perhaps different to many others, as I strive to always do the best for the horse physically and mentally. My goal is to work with my horse today in a way that will keep him as happy and healthy as possible during his entire life.

But right now, in some areas people are taught that three years old, or even younger if the horse was quite big, was the correct age to start a horse and get it working.

I got an email in recently from a lady in the US.

This lady told me that she had purchased her horse when he was 4 years old. When he was 5 ½ he had bucked her off badly. Suspecting that something was wrong she had a bone scan and ultrasound examination carried out. Without going into too much detail, significant problems were found - her horse had physical issues including damage to bones and arthritis. He had been 'broken' at 3 years old and ridden a lot since then. Although she blamed herself for riding him too much, she's not alone in that and was unaware of the possible implications. Many of us have grown up with horses in an environment where it's expected for horses to be in full work at a young age and even out competing. This lady loves her horse and is doing everything she can to help him.

Homework:

Talk to at least 3 friends. Ask them what age they think is the earliest a horse's body is fully physically mature.

The rollercoaster

It's important to talk about a big issue many riders have. It's the dramatic and emotional rollercoaster of owning a horse. One day you're on top of the world after a blissful ride with your horse in the arena. You felt connected and carefree, and your horse was confident and relaxed. It felt like magic. But the next day, there was a gale outside, your horse spooked at everything, ignored your attempts to ask them to relax, stood on your foot (ouch) which then turned black and green, leaving you no choice but to abandon the session in tears and hobble home dejectedly.

- Or maybe your horse is lame one morning and has something wrong with a hoof.
- Or someone says something unkind to you, because you're doing groundwork instead of riding your horse.
- Or you got a new horse you're struggling to connect with.
- Or you find a melanoma on your horse and burst into tears :(
- Or you asked too much of your horse, your horse lost confidence and you feel like a failure.
- Or you had a bad fall and feel sick at the thought of riding.
- Maybe time is an issue. Not everyone has the luxury of spending an hour or more daily with your horse. So you beat yourself up about this internally.

It happens to all of us, because our horses mean so much to us. A bad day, a health worry, a scary situation, a loss of confidence, a tumble, a judgement, a criticism from someone else… things like this can literally turn your world upside down. This is the emotional rollercoaster of owning a horse. It's intense and it's soul wrenching at times. You're not alone. We all struggle. We all have to deal with grief, anxiety and confidence issues at different times. We all make mistakes.

I think the biggest mistake we can make is not trying.

"I went from dreading going to the barn to loving going to the barn. Having Elaine's resources to guide me and give me a framework has been a Godsend". Doris, Canada.

Our horses have so much potential to be the horse of our dreams. They want to connect with us. They want to have that trusting relationship with us, but our fear of making a mistake can cause us to literally self-sabotage.

If you have a good heart and you always want to do the best for your horse, and if you combine that with being patient and going slowly, you are 100% on the right path. A huge part of horsemanship is about surviving the rollercoaster and having great friends to support us when we need their help.

While many people own horses, we are all on a different path. I know from personal experience that it can be difficult to find those who are on a similar journey to us, but when we do, those friendships we make can be priceless.

Homework:

Join our Facebook community at www.starthorselistening.com

Groundwork and in hand exercises

What is groundwork and in hand work?

Groundwork and in hand work are two similar terms that describe any training we do with the horse that does not involve a rider. These terms also include any time we look to develop a connection with a horse which does not include riding as part of this connection.

Doing groundwork with your horse can cover lots of different situations including:

- Walking out to the field to put a halter on your horse.
- Leading your haltered horse back from the field to the stable.
- Grooming your horse to clean and also massage them.
- Asking your horse to do any type of exercises while you walk close to or beside your horse.
- Asking your horse to move at any speed in any direction while you are connected to them via a lead rope or similar.

- Placing a pattern of poles on the ground and asking your horse to walk, trot or canter over them. Doing exercises with poles are often called 'polework exercises'.
- Connecting with your horse while they are loose in the field or arena, and have nothing on their head. This is called liberty work or liberty training.
- Walking side by side with your horse, with the horse at 'liberty' (no halter on the horse, and the horse is free to leave at any time).

I regularly do groundwork exercises with my horses. Groundwork exercises are very useful for a number of reasons, they:

- Increase your awareness about your horse's state of mind.
- Build a connection and partnership with your horse.
- Help your horse to build confidence in new places.
- Help your horse to build confidence with scary objects like umbrellas and bicycles.
- Help build your own confidence.
- Identify potential health issues or lameness.
- Identify situations where your horse is likely to lose confidence before you ride them.
- Help you to get to know your horse better.
- Encourage you to spend time with a young horse, retired horse or a non-ridden equine.
- Introduce and teach new exercises of all types, that you will repeat later in the saddle.
- Help you to see how all four feet move. This makes it easier to ask your horse to move a specific leg at the moment which it would be easiest for the horse to accomplish, which is often called 'getting in time with the feet'.
- Introduce a horse to a saddle and bridle for the first time.
- Have you spend time with your horse if you are unable to ride for a period of time.

"I bought my Connemara Becky in December 2020. From the start she had mounting block issues and seemed to be scared of everything. I worked with her to build her confidence through

walking and groundwork and soon realised she wasn't actually scared of everything, she was just scared of being somewhere new without anything familiar. The groundwork built trust between us but the mounting problems got worse, until in March 2021, Becky threw me off and wouldn't allow me to ride her anymore. People told me she was 'just being naughty' and I should be 'firmer with her' but because by now I was listening to her through our groundwork, I realised she wasn't naughty but must be in pain. Finally my chiropractor found the answer - Becky's back and withers were seized up and she had pain in her pelvis. He treated her, and now she is no longer spooky, and she will stand happily at the mounting block for me to get on and ride her. The groundwork we did as part of Elaine's course gave me the confidence to listen to the horse rather than to other people, to stop riding her when she knew she couldn't be ridden, and to keep searching to find the answer to what was worrying her. Groundwork has helped us to build a really strong bond of trust and partnership, which I know will now also benefit our ridden work." Annetta, UK.

Given the many proven benefits of groundwork, it's still remarkable that most horse riders do not do enough groundwork with their horses! Rosie, one of my students from the UK, summed it all up in very few words.

"I don't mean to be cliche here, but groundwork has literally helped every single aspect of my relationship with my horse."

The groundwork exercises in this book are recommended for horses over the age of 3. As horses are only physically mature between 5.5 and 6.5 years of age or older (some horses can continue to grow for another year or two more after that) we don't want to ask our horses to do too much at an early age.

10 minute lessons and bad weather exercises

Groundwork exercises are great when you're short on time, when it's too hot to do much, or during the winter when the ground may be slippery.

You don't need to ride your horse, so all you need to do is grab a halter and you're good to go. Some of my favourite groundwork exercises can be done in 10 minutes, are fun for both the horse and human and many only require the horse to walk or stand still - so they are perfect for when the ground is icy or it's too cold or hot to do too much work.

Doris lives in Canada and gets a lot of snow each winter!

"The pole work exercises are helping Chester to lift his lazy feet. I put the poles in the snow now and again as well, so he really has to lift himself as he passes over the poles. At a trot, it is especially nice to watch him lift his whole belly up along with those feet. It is definitely something I would recommend to anyone who is seeking to do something interesting from the ground. It isn't just what it does for him physically - it is also what it is doing for our relationship. It's very worthwhile." Doris, Canada.

Are these groundwork exercises for you?

The groundwork exercises which are covered in this book are suitable for:

- Trail riders
- Dressage riders
- People who do not do dressage
- Western riders
- English riders
- Vaquero horsemanship followers (a wonderful riding tradition from California)
- Natural horsemanship students
- Anyone who wishes to build better connection and partnership with their horse
- New horses
- All healthy horses over 3 years of age.

"Starting a new relationship with a horse is exciting, wonderful, daunting and scary all at the same time and that is where I found myself with Sir George, an 11 year old beautiful Appaloosa gelding. I cannot express how much the Confidence Fix and ground work exercises have helped me to build a solid and trusting relationship with my new horse. From the first few weeks, walking out in hand, pole work exercises and recognising body language all contributed to George finding trust in us, looking to us for guidance and above all communicating with us and us with him. Now we are 6 months in and our bond has grown. We still have work to do but now we are on this journey together! And that is thanks to Elaine!" Katie, UK.

The #1 lead rope mistake to avoid

Liberty work is a type of groundwork which is done with your horse while there is no halter or any type of equipment on their head. It's a lot of fun and a great way to spend time with your horse.

Online groundwork is done while your horse is wearing a halter on their head and you are holding the lead rope. It includes a very wide range of exercises that will help you handle your horse and also prepare you for riding.

There is one huge mistake you want to avoid as much as you can. You do not want to pull on that lead rope. This sounds simple, but it's quite difficult to do.

It's a bit like going shopping.

When I go to a supermarket to get groceries I usually have a long list! So instead of getting a smaller basket to carry everything, I go over to the trolleys, put in a €2 euro coin, take the large trolly out of the rack, and then push the trolley ahead of me as I walk into the supermarket.

The important word here is push.

Imagine your horse is a supermarket trolley. When you work with them online, have a try at pushing them forwards and away from you on an arc. You want to try to avoid using the lead rope to pull them forwards or sideways, but instead use the tail of the rope or a signal from your hand to push them away. Don't stick your hand out to the side in the direction that you want to go. Think in terms of stepping towards and moving the shoulder away then allowing your horse forward. It's a big concept, but it's the best first step is one that everyone can work on.

Anytime you are doing groundwork and you are holding the lead rope in your hand I want you to notice how many times during your session that the lead rope became even slightly tight. When this happens it causes lots of issues, including helping the horse to lose balance, unintentionally asking the horse to walk into your space and creating worry and tension in the horse's body. Most horses respond to being pulled on by pulling back or leaning into the pressure, which is the opposite of the softness you are aiming for.

Most horse owners tell me they never pull on their horses. However when you look at a video or even a photo, you can see that the rope between their horse's head and their hand is straight. It may only be a tiny pressure, but it is a pull. It's like a silent disease that most people aren't aware of. Once we become aware of this habit, then we can work on changing it.

Not pulling on the lead rope will improve your horse's balance, confidence and athletic ability. It will also help you and your horse to truly "feel" for each other.

We need to be consistent to be fair on our horses. When we learn the lesson of 'don't pull' it needs to be part of our daily lives. So many times I've watched people working with their horse in the arena, carefully focusing on softness, balance and never pulling. Then when the session is over they turn to the gate and the slack goes out of the rope as they head towards it… Make never pulling your lesson for life and your horse will love you for it!

"Elaine said, "Don't pull on your horse's lead rope". So I stopped. It never occurred to me how rude I've been! Hey, Mrs. Fuzzy, I'm going to treat you like luggage. Yank! Our time together is all about what I want to get done. Yank!

Instead, if I find I want to change our direction, or do something different, I slow way down to see if my horse is coming with me. If not, I turn back to my horse and tell her of my change of plans. I may lay my palm on some part of her and ask for what I want then Wait.For.Her.Reply!
How novel! Just as if I respect her and want her to be in on this horsemanship journey with me!

One of my horses, Penny, has a recurring eye infection I've been treating again until the vet comes out in a couple days *fingers crossed*. Penny has always been (human interpretation) rather grumpy and head tossy and biting the lead rope and pushy. But I've treated her eye three times a day and every time she still comes up to me in their 13 acre paddock and field.

A surprise benefit is that I'm really getting to know Penny, even after all these years by interpreting things from her point of view. Another benefit is that Penny is getting to know me and that I'm not just another dope on the other end of the rope. I'm a dope who truly cares about her.

Feeling comfortable and confident handling my horses has always seemed fleeting. That things had to go a "certain way" or I'd be undone and lose my nerve, then have to force myself to *whatever*. Sure there has been less drama over the years, but it honestly hasn't been a lot of fun. It's been heartbreaking in all honesty.

But now I have a better way to be with my horses. Not a technique but an overarching principle that is learned through simple but really thoughtful exercises. I can have fun, be with my horse in all their moods and keep my confidence because I'm not trying to "get them to do something", we are learning together. Thank you Elaine" Joan.

The no pull exercise

Lead your horse for one minute going various directions and speeds. Ask them to turn right and left and to stand still and then walk on again. Observe how many times you inadvertently pull on your horse.

Leading your horse & creating partnership

I always recommend that we walk by our horse's shoulder when leading them. There is this argument that if you walk by the shoulder it isn't as safe as walking in front. Pay your money and take your choice... but my reason for saying to be by the shoulder is that I teach my horses not to barge their shoulders into me. I make sure that I can control the shoulder and move my horse's shoulder away if I need to. Of course we can be barged by a worried horse - but if a horse decides that something is really frightening they can do a number of things, including running forward into a person in front. We just do the best we can to prepare to be safe.

So why do I say lead from the shoulder? First of all, when doing basic groundwork, we learn to control and move our horse's shoulders, so that they don't push on to us or crowd us with their shoulders. We also learn to work with some distance between us, avoiding putting a pull on the rope. Then we take that learning and apply it when we are leading our horses, be it just to their paddock, or out on a long walk in the countryside.

When we walk by their shoulder, we are close to where we would sit when riding. So the way that we use our rope to move our horse will be very similar to how we would use our reins from the saddle. We also learn to encourage our horses forward without pulling on them. We might use our voice, our energy, or encourage some forward motion with the rope or a flag. No point in trying to pull them forward because we can't do that when we're riding!

Pretty much everything I teach is setting us up for more advanced groundwork that will then prepare us and our horses for work in the saddle. So to move a horse out on to a circle I would move the shoulder, then allow them forward. I would not stick my arm out and effectively put a feel on the rope that would pull them towards me. To do lateral work we need to move the shoulder and body rather than concentrate on the head. So that's reflected when leading - everything is consistent for the horse.

I had a chat about this with a good friend Kas Fitzpatrick, who is an experienced and talented horse person. Here are her thoughts.

"I really enjoy walking with my horses, it's such a pleasure to spend relaxing time with them. I always walk by their shoulder, unless we are maybe dealing with an obstacle. People talk about wanting a partnership with their horse then they walk along out front dragging their horse behind them. Partners walk hand in hand. My horses and I walk side by side together, looking forward to what's ahead. I love that connection, when out on a walk with my horse, to be able to just put out a hand and touch him gently on the neck."

As you progress in your training it's good to learn how to lead your horse from pretty much anywhere - in front, by the head, the shoulder, the belly and even from behind. To start with however I recommend that you and your horse get good walking together with you at the shoulder.

Groundwork tools

Any tools and equipment we use with our horses must fit correctly, be made well and cause no discomfort to the horse. Many horses with pain show no obvious signs, so it is up to the horse owner to be very mindful to be on the lookout for any potential pain issues or changes of behaviour that may indicate pain.

Halter and lead rope

I use a well made rope halter attached to a 12 foot rope. Rope halters come in different sizes so it's important to get one that fits your horse and is of good quality.

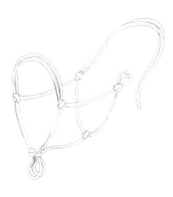

I do not use lead ropes with metal clips on them. The metal clip distorts the signal between your hand on one end of the rope and your horse's sensitive face on the other. It can also bang on your horse's jaw. Instead I use a lead rope with a simple loop that I can use to attach to the halter.

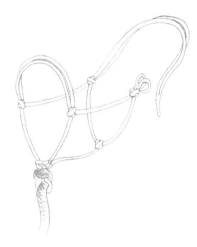

When the halter is on the horse the nose band should lie about half way between the end of the horse's eye and the point where the nostril begins. If the nose band on the halter is lower than this it will be resting on delicate cartilage rather than bone. The risk is that it will impede the horse's breathing and cause them pain. So fit is extremely important.

There is a specific way to tie the halter that avoids the knot tightening or becoming hard to undo.

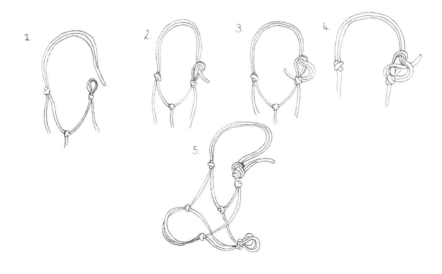

A rope halter is not like a leather headcollar. A rope halter will not break. So you should never tie a horse up to anything solid (like a fence, a gate or a trailer) while he is wearing a rope halter. You should never ask a horse to travel in a trailer while wearing a rope halter. A rope halter should only be used on a horse when there is a human holding a lead rope and watching the horse at all times. Many people suggest the importance of carrying a pen knife in case there is an emergency and you ever need to cut the halter to free the horse.

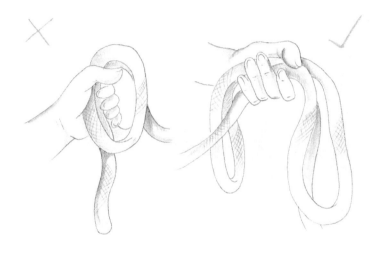

When you are holding any lead rope it is very important for safety reasons that you never wrap it around your hand. Instead, coil up the lead rope and hold the coils in your hand, or fold the lead up once or twice and hold the folds. That way if the rope gets pulled through your hand it won't tighten around your hand causing injury or even possibly result in you being dragged along.

The halter fit exercise

- Check that your halter fits your horse.
- Check there is not a clip on your lead rope.
- Check you can attach rope to the halter without making the halter tight (see diagram above).
- Check you are tying the knot correctly.
- Check the lead rope is not circled around your hand when leading

Confidence training

Confidence is the first step on the ladder for both you and your horse. Every goal you want to accomplish with your horse will be significantly easier if both you and your horse feel confident.

If you have a new horse you want to build a connection with, a young horse who needs help developing confidence, or an anxious horse who lacks confidence, choosing to spend some weeks or months building confidence is the most valuable thing you can do.

"I'd just like to share how proud I am of my little horse and how glad I am that I changed my attitude to listening to the horse. It's thanks to the fact that all I've done is hang out with her and groom her and massage her that she totally accepted the mounting block and accepted me leaning over her back. She didn't bother at all!

This girl is from a very unpleasant previous home and it's such a wonderful experience to have a lovely relationship with her. And just now I said to her "I need to put some cream on your bum" so she turned round and gave me her bum!! It's so lovely! I'm so glad I'm not feeling pressured to rush her into doing anything which is what I would have done before joining this community and doing the workshops." Grace

Many riders also reach a plateau with the horses. Many times the cause of this plateau is a lack of confidence in the horse or rider.

A few months ago I met a lady in Australia who had a horse who was very worried and anxious. He would get very bothered on trail rides and it was quite an issue. She committed to spending twelve months doing as much as she could with him to build confidence, including travelling to one multi-day clinic every four weeks. I met her when her year was nearly over. She said that many people who knew both her and her horse could not believe it was the same horse. He was so calm and relaxed, fine in new places and now loved going on trips and adventures!

Sometimes if we feel we have plateaued in our riding and we haven't seen a lot of improvement, this can be related to missing foundations. Confidence is one of the most important foundations that every horse needs in order to be able to achieve their best. If you have any confidence issues yourself you need a plan to improve your confidence as well. Horse riding and owning a horse is supposed to be fun! It is not supposed to be something that gives you anxiety. If you are in this situation, there is a lot of hope.

Benefits of a confident horse and rider

Here are some of the useful benefits to building confidence in you and your horse.

- It's so much easier to teach your horse new things.
- The horse can learn faster as they are focused on you.
- A confident horse is much less likely to spook or jump sideways when you are riding or leading them on the ground.
- Working with a confident horse is much safer than working with an anxious and potentially unpredictable horse.
- If you feel confident with your horse it's much easier for you to learn.
- You will enjoy your time with your horse more.
- You will be safer as you can be focused on your horse and listening to them, instead of being worried or anxious.

Many years ago when I bought my Connemara, Ozzie, back from the horse sales in Kilkenny, he was scared of everything. He was scared of all humans - including me. He was scared of saddles, bridles, numnahs, bits, girths, the buckles on the girths that jingle unexpectedly, random noises, sudden noises, poles on the ground, people close to him, people far away in the distance…

The list went on and on and on.

Leading him took courage as there were a lot of spooks and hard to predict fast sideways jumps. It was actually quite dangerous to lead him. It was impossible to go out on a trail ride with him, it just wasn't an option.

Then we have Matilda, my Irish sports horse. When I got Matilda as a five year old she was herd bound and scared of being without another horse. She was excellent at spooking when you were leading her. She believed that any birds who jumped out of a tree or a bush were about to kill her.

Let's be honest here. If you have a horse who spooks suddenly, very fast, quite often and when you are not expecting it - either when you are leading them on foot or riding them - you're going to lose confidence. It might feel like all you're trying to do is just stay alive. I think all horse people have been there at some point so don't beat yourself up. There are things you can do to help you and your horse.

I know one way to try and deal with the confidence issue before you ride is to lunge your horse and work through excess energy before you get into the saddle, but that can create more issues. Is it really fixing the actual problem? Or are you just trying to stick a band aid on something? Because in a few days you'll probably just have to do it again. What I've noticed is that it's not necessarily good for the horse physically - a horse can be looking out of the circle and not balanced on the circle - that it can worry the horse mentally and it's not a good physical pattern for long term health.

In terms of partnership and communication I feel lunging can often teach the horse to zone you out and pretty much ignore you, apart from during the moments you ask them to change speed or direction. That's 100% the opposite of what we want to teach our horses to do. We want to help our horses focus on us, not teach them to ignore us!

In so many cases the #1 thing I see that stops us making progress together is a lack of confidence in horse or rider or usually both.

There is one good thing that I want to mention - often if we can build confidence in the horse the rider's confidence will also grow naturally. I want to introduce two groundwork strategies that I use which will help you to build confidence with your horse and make your time together a lot more enjoyable.

Walking in hand with your horse

One really powerful strategy is to complete a series of simple yet powerful groundwork exercises, with the goal to walk anything between 10 and 100 miles with your horse, over a time period that is realistic for you.

For example, most people could walk a mile in between 15 to 20 minutes.

And it takes about 2,000 steps to walk a mile.

So if you were to walk with your horse for one hour, you would have walked a little over 3 miles, and taken over 6000 steps.

If you walk your horse for one hour, once a week for a year, then you would have walked over 150 miles!

1 hour of walking a week with your horse x 52 weeks in a year = 156 miles.

Now, obviously there is a little more to it than just putting a halter on your horse and setting off into the sunset! It's common to have some issues you need to fix first. These are the 6 most common horse situations I regularly see:

- The slow horse sets out at snail's pace, You'll find that even if you increase your energy then you're dragging him and he still doesn't speed up.
- The fast horse who takes big steps (or a lot of steps quickly!) and the result is that they are leaving you behind. How can you teach them to mirror your speed and slow down?
- The herd bound horse who finds confidence when they are with their herd mates. But when you take them away on their own, it all goes pear-shaped!
- The hungry horse. What do you do if you are leading your horse with lead rope and they put their head down to try to eat grass every few steps? This is a really common issue I see a lot.
- The worried horse who spooks dramatically when a bird flies out of a tree. This is a fast way to lose confidence and end up in a dangerous situation.
- The pushy horse who walks into your personal space uninvited? And one day you think they might just knock you over?

To achieve their 5 mile, 10 mile or even 100 mile walking goal many of our students found that the secret to success was to first spend time working on simple but specific ground work exercises. These simple exercises put the foundations in place to prepare horses and people to begin their 100 miles! They were the starting point that would help people to solve the six issues listed above.

The good news is that you don't need access to miles of trails to be able to help your horse build confidence.

You just need where your horse lives now. This could be a stable or yard area, safe roadway, paddocks, arena or a field or two. This approach uses the comfort zone model to slowly but effectively build confidence in your horse.

This is exactly what Annetta did with her horse Becky.

"Becky was brilliant today! We've been working on walking in hand. We passed all her scary things - bike, four dogs (one off lead accompanying bike), four vans and a truck. She used to shake, rear and run off the road. Now after three weeks of walking in hand, she is getting really confident. I am really proud of her!" Annetta, UK.

Michelle from the UK also found that putting in the work on the ground was just what she and her pony needed.

"We had a few issues last year with going forward and not being a partnership. We spent most of winter walking together and then 3 weeks ago I realised Diamond really needs to do increasing exercise for her health. So I put on my brave pants, got in the saddle, took a deep breath and off we went, she has been perfect. She's responsive and aware of what's going on around her, but her ears are constantly swivelling around to listen to me also. I barely have to use my leg aids, she's taking encouragement from my voice as she does from the ground. She's brave and curious, and wants to explore different tracks. I never thought I'd be the girl riding one handed through the woods, chatting away to my horse and enjoying

the view and the birds. I accredit all of this to the miles of in hand walking we've done together the past few months. I have ended up with a trail riding pony." Michelle, UK.

The one mile exercise

Walk 1 mile in hand with your horse, in an area where they feel safe. If they only feel safe in a small paddock, or any small area, then walk 1 mile by doing laps of that area. As our goal is to build confidence, do not ask your horse to walk in an area where he will be anxious or worried.

Creating a confidence 'to do' list

The second strategy I recommend to build confidence is to make a list of all the things you can use to help your horse to feel braver. It can include plastic bags, bicycles, cows, umbrellas and lots more objects and situations! Now this list is going to be long. In fact, the longer the better. Literally write down a huge list of everything you can think of.

When your list is complete, pick out a safe environment for where you can work with your horse. Working on the ground, very slowly introduce one thing from your list that your horse might feel is a bit scary.

The closer the scary thing is to the horse, the more likely they are to panic. The further away the scary thing is from them the less likely they are to feel anxious. So start by having the scary object quite a distance away from your horse.

You should always start by standing between the horse and the scary thing. That way, if your horse jumps away unexpectedly from the scary thing they also jump away from you and not on top of you.

You want to stand there quietly and notice when the horse feels confident. You can tell this from their body language. Their body looks calm and relaxed. They are breathing normally and they change their focus regularly.

The exact distance required between your horse and the scary object is 100% determined solely by your horse.

- You may own a horse who needs to be 100 metres away from an umbrella on day 1. This horse might take 5 short sessions, over 5 days, to finally be confident enough to stand beside the umbrella.
- You may own a horse who needs to be 50 metres away from an umbrella on day 1. And this horse might take 3 short sessions, over 3 days, to finally be confident enough to stand beside the umbrella.

The time needed and the distance required is chosen by the horse. In order to build confidence we need to be aware of their preferences and facilitate the speed and distance the horse requires during this process. When building confidence the horse decides the distance and speed. The human does not.

Does this sound familiar? Remember the magic of comfort zones?

- The comfort zone
- The not sure zone
- The danger zone

You should apply the theory of comfort zones when introducing your horse to things that worry them.

A friend of mine in England had to introduce her horse to a vibrating back pad to help him with some issues he was having. She decided to let him know what was coming and switch it on, then approach him. At first she thought she'd never get it on him, his 'comfort zone' (where he stayed relaxed) was as wide as the yard - maybe 20 metres away! But working gently, gradually in and out of the 'not so safe zone', he allowed his comfort zone to grow, and after a couple of days he was able to have the pad on his back. At which point he realised he loved it and fell asleep in the sun!

The goal with our horses is to help them change how they feel, from fear to curiosity. When we do that it completely changes their behaviour. I love when my horses become curious, because they actually start to build their confidence. Not only are you creating confidence in your horse, but you're building trust and partnership as well. Confidence building lessons can become really fun and enjoyable for you and your horse.

The confidence exercise

Make a list of all the things you would like your horse to be confident with.

#1 Confidence mistake to avoid

There is a buzzword in various circles today and it's all about 'desensitisation'.

Many horse riders want to desensitise their horses, in order to reduce the chance that their horse will do any type of unexpected or sudden movement. The last thing I want for my horse is to help them to become less sensitive! If I want to help my horse become a beautiful riding horse I need to keep as much sensitivity in the horse as I can. Because later I will want my horse to be able to move from the tiniest cues and signals that I use.

If I've trained my horse to be insensitive I am shooting myself in the foot. I am actually going to create a problem that I will need to spend time trying to fix in the future.

"Six days ago, I was at the verge of selling my horse Summer. I saw no way to fix his "spooking" and lack of confidence. My husband had a buyer but I kept telling him, "I have to talk to my horse first" and so I prayed for an answer. I found Elaine's Confidence Workshop for horses via Facebook, and it was free! I had already invested in other horsemanship programs that were promising, but were either too time consuming, or never spoke to my heart or made a difference in me understanding my horse. Now I plan to keep working on building confidence with Summer and myself; and no, he is not for sale!" Sarah, USA.

I believe working on a strategy to build confidence in the horse is the best policy. You may not believe me yet, so let me explain.

Most people try to 'desensitise' their horses, either gradually or worse than that by just forcing them to go through situations when they are too scared to think. Maybe they are out on the trail riding and their horse gets worried. So they start kicking them and putting a lot of pressure on their horse to walk forwards. Sure, they may eventually force their horse to walk on, but their horse has lost confidence, has learned that the rider doesn't care when he feels worried. While the situation has been resolved from the rider's perspective - trust has been eroded for the horse. Then they wonder why their horse is still spooky on trail rides. As long as they continue to not listen to the horse the situation will never be properly resolved. They need to learn to allow their horse to choose.

We don't want to desensitise our horses, or turn them into heavy, switched-off and dull equines. A horse can only be responsive if they are sensitive. Instead we use the 'Confidence Learning' technique to build confidence in the horse, protecting their natural lightness, curiosity and softness. We do it in a way that is kind to the horse.

"My horse's name is Mia and she is 5 years old at the end of the month. Mia was not very confident, partly due to being young and having a new owner. I bought her as my first horse 8 months ago. This affected my future plans for us together. Mia has massively gained in confidence, which has increased my confidence, when being with her. We have greater trust in each other and our connection is improving. Before Elaine's help, Mia would rear when she was scared, which reduced my confidence. Now I understand more about her body language and how to improve her confidence using safety zones, she has gained confidence and been making her safety zones larger, which has helped me gain confidence with her. Elaine's lessons have made me think of sessions with my horse differently, and following this confidence training has improved our relationship together." Chelsea, Wales, UK.

Homework:

Write 2 unwanted results you might see after desensitizing a horse.

#2 Confidence mistake to avoid

There is one thing that I must talk about when we are thinking about teaching a horse to be confident. This is an approach to training called 'Flooding'.

Flooding is a technique that involves forcing the horse into a situation where it is close to something that it is afraid of and unable to move away from it.

Some trainers, and horse owners, will use this method deliberately in the belief that the horse will be scared for a while, then they will calm down and accept the thing they are scared of and the problem is solved. They belong to the 'leave them to get over it' school of thought. It is an unkind way to treat any animal and can be dangerous:

- The horse can panic so much that it hurts itself before the trainer can intervene.
- Flooding induces a state known as 'learned helplessness', where the horse appears to accept the situation but in fact has really just shut down.
- In some situations flooding can ultimately make the situation worse, with the horse becoming even more scared by the object that worried them and less able to accept it.

Say my horse was afraid of plastic bottles and I wanted to get them to accept them. I could lay a couple of bottles down in the arena and allow the horse to freely approach them from a safe distance in their comfort zone with me by their side. I would let my horse go as close as they wanted to, but also to move away to think if they needed to, then go back. That approach would be working with the horse's nature and gradually building their confidence.

If I took my horse who was afraid of plastic bottles and put their saddle on, then tied the plastic bottles to the saddle and let him loose - that would be flooding. If I did that to Ozzie when he first came to me I think it would have been a very long time before I could go near him again!

The problem with flooding is that in many cases it appears to 'work' so people continue to teach and recommend it. It's not kind or sympathetic to the nature of horses and it's not an approach that any behaviourist I know would support.

Homework:

Share 2 situations where people flood their horses. Share how you think the horse would feel about each situation.

Herd bound and barn sour

About two years ago I was hosting a clinic in Ireland. I was riding Matilda at the clinic and she was doing really well. There was one small issue that was going on the whole time. Matilda was a little herd bound to Ozzie. This meant that instead of thinking about me, she was thinking about Ozzie. She was mentally bound to her herd. She would have much preferred to go back outside to Ozzie! While we were able to work on new things together I could often feel that slight drag back towards the gate that led out to the paddock and Ozzie. It was small - but it was influencing our balance and causing her to drift a little towards the gate while we were riding.

I'd rather my horse be with me - and not mentally with another horse in a distant paddock. To look at Matilda you probably wouldn't have noticed the issue, but I felt it. After 2 days of this I really wanted to fix it. I decided that on the 3rd morning of the clinic I would get up really early and Matilda and I would do a session together in the arena at 7.30am, before anyone else had arrived to feed their horses. So I dragged myself out of bed at 6.30 am (on the last day of a clinic when I am usually happy but exhausted!) checked on all the visitors' horses, and fed my horses as the sun began to rise. It was warm and there wasn't a cloud in the sky. It was a magical and still morning.

I put Matilda's halter on, and we walked together into the arena. I wasn't expecting much to be honest. She was not hugely herd bound, but it had been a noticeable small thing over the last 2 days. My plan was to improve it just a little, and be happy with any sort of progress. As we were going to be riding all day I just wanted to do about 20 minutes with her and to keep things easy and fun. I put a halter on Matilda and walked her in.

There was a special feeling that morning inside the arena. The early morning sun had flooded all over the sand and the entire arena looked like a perfectly lit movie set. I decided the best way to build a little connection together and have fun would be to try some liberty work together. It would definitely tell me if she was herd bound - in which case I predicted she would just stay by the gate and wish she was back out in the paddock with Ozzie!

But no.

Matilda looked directly at me and said:

'"Elaine, what are we going to do together?"

"Let's try some liberty Matilda! I think you'll like it and we can move together like a team."

"Sounds good Elaine, show me how to do it!"

So that morning as the sun rose across Ireland and everyone was still asleep in bed, Matilda and I danced at liberty around that arena. It was one of those special moments you can have with your horse. One of those times when they are totally focused on you, every step you make is mirrored by them - and you feel this almost magical thought connection between you both.

I was blown away. It was not what I had expected at all! At liberty, we were able to walk, stop, turn, backup and trot together - side by side. It was the coolest feeling in the world!

About 20 minutes after we started I told her she was wonderful, unlatched the gate and led her back out to the paddock. We took every step together. I was grateful I knew some liberty exercises that I was able to use to help her understand also and to build that connection.

The herd bound issue

Sometimes when a horse is low on confidence it shows up because they don't want to leave their horse friends. If you take them away from their horse friends they panic. Or maybe they refuse to leave the other horses. Or their friend leaves their paddock and they start galloping around and panicking. Or you can't take your horse out alone on a trail ride because he will panic too much when he is away from his friends.

This is called being barn sour or herd bound. It is a really common issue with horses and understandable as they are herd animals and that is where they feel secure. It can be a major safety issue, and it can stop you from doing a lot of fun stuff with your horse. It stems from a lack of confidence.

One of the most effective ways I've found to help a herd bound horse is to use the one step at a time method. You are looking to take them one step further away from their friend, and then bring them back again.

At the start, you need to first identify where your horse starts to get worried. It is leaving the paddock? It is walking 10 steps away after leaving the paddock? It is walking 50 steps away after leaving the paddock? It is going out of sight of the other horses?

We are using comfort zones again. Our goal is to ask our horse to move an extra step or two away from their friend, just enough so they are in their 'not sure' zone, but then to bring them back to their comfort zone.

But we do not want to take out horses far enough away that they go into the danger zone.

Originally when I got Matilda, when I took her out of the paddock she would worry. So instead of taking her away further, I would ask her to walk a little doing laps on the other side of the gate. After a minute or two, Ozzie would go back to eating grass in the paddock, and Matilda would relax and realise that everything was fine.

Then after a few minutes, I would end the session and put her back into the paddock.

The next day I did this and noticed that she calmed down much faster when I took her out of the paddock. We repeated the same exercise, doing a little work just outside the paddock, and she was happy. After following the process over a few days I was soon able to take her out of the paddock and walk her around in a larger space next door, without worrying either her or Ozzie.

It's not a fast process, but building a relationship with a horse and helping them to develop confidence rarely is. However it is a process that works, and by applying the comfort zone model it maximises your chances of success with your horse.

Homework:

Rate how herd bound your horse is. 0 = not herd bound at all. 10 = very herd bound.

Liberty work and partnership building

I live in Ireland, and in the winter it is freezing! Right now as I type there is snow on the ground, the temperature hasn't been much above freezing in over two weeks and I have to break the ice on the water troughs each morning.

Ugh. I'm not really a winter girl!

The question is - what on earth do you do with your horse in bad weather?

Aside from keeping them happy, fed and watered, I actually like to use the cold weather to my advantage. In the summer I tend to focus more on riding. Trail rides, wandering around with my horse in the sunshine, doing lateral maneuvers in the big field beside the pond... it's all lovely.

However in the winter I'm wrapped up in gloves, a scarf and two coats. With the dark evenings and cold weather - it's unlikely I'm going to ride each day (yup, not a hope!). I even got one of those fancy electric jackets a few years ago. Even in awful weather I still want to keep that connection with my horses. To do this I focus on simple liberty sessions that can be done in under 15 minutes, once or twice a week. This way I can keep working with my horses, even during January in Ireland! I don't feel bad we've done almost nothing in months due to hard ground or snow - because we are still able to spend a little time together each week.

Liberty work involves spending time with your horse when you are not riding your horse. There is no halter or any equipment on your horse. Your horse is free to move in any direction any time he or she chooses.

Liberty exercises are so much fun. They are a quick and easy way to connect with your horse - in any weather! Then once the spring arrives with better weather, we can get back to a lot more riding and fun activities.

There may be snow and ice on the ground, but if you are looking to keep that connection I think liberty exercises are a great option. In the winter I love to spice things up and focus on 'bad weather' friendly exercises like groundwork, liberty work, polework, and walking on foot with my horses. It's fine for your horses to take things a bit easier and have a break from being ridden. You don't need an arena for liberty work, you don't even need a very big space. One of my friends does simple liberty exercises in a 12x12 stable!

" Liberty is a great option for Mickey and myself. We do obstacles, groundwork, and play with the big ball. We feel connected and yet free when we play at liberty. Last week we were walking and trotting together in the pasture and I asked for a trotting circle around me. He did both directions without being asked! There was abundant grass in the pasture which he doesn't get a lot of but he chose me!" Susie, USA.

Here's one weird belief that is 100% not true - it is the belief that we should feel guilty about not riding our horses enough. I think it's important to give the horses a bit of a break. To me that means giving them a rest from riding a few times each week. So I don't feel guilty about it. If you are in a similar position, you shouldn't either.

Liberty work means having some form of communication or connection with a horse when the horse doesn't have any tack on. So there is no halter or headcollar. The horse is loose or free, in an arena, paddock or field. The horse is free to move away from you if they want. It's about allowing your horse the gift of choice. Doing liberty work is a super way to improve your body language skills - to learn what your horse likes and dislikes, to build a connection and improve your partnership together.

"Our liberty journey has only just begun but I have already learnt so much about my relationship with Sir George. We are half way through Elaine's program and I am so much more aware of George's communication, body language and reactions. He relishes in grooming and scratches and loves the shadowing exercises and good surprises in the shape of unexpected apples in the field! I feel like I have a totally new way of working with horses now and almost as if I'm finally communicating in their language." Katie, UK

Benefits of liberty work:

- Super for bad weather or when the ground is hard and it's not safe to go faster than a walk.
- Great if you only have 15 mins to do something with your horse.
- Perfect for winter exercises.
- Useful to build connection and trust without riding your horse

"Watching a horse and human work together in a partnership has always caught my eye. I've had an interest in doing liberty work with my horse someday. However, my situation is a little different. I have a medical condition called Arthrogryposis that causes me to be limited to a walker or wheelchair. My condition limits me to what groundwork and riding I can do with my horse. I felt like my horse and I had a great connection from the start, but I wanted to grow that bond with my horse..... so that is why I started liberty.

I am new to liberty training and am still learning. So far I am loving it! My horse and I have progressed so much since we've started. I feel like our bond is getting stronger and that my horse trusts me more. I love to be independent, and that is another reason why I love liberty; I can do it with my horse independently with no one's help. I believe that liberty training will also strengthen our bond while in the saddle too. My horse is my best friend and I want to have the strongest bond possible." Jewell, USA.

Liberty exercise

Walk side by side with your horse for 3 or more steps, while your horse is at liberty. The goal is for your feet to sync up with your horse's front feet.

"The liberty exercises have helped me slow down and think about what I am doing. It has helped my horses because I am watching and learning from them." Beth USA

Magic corner exercise

When we work with our horses, either on the ground or in the saddle, it's very useful to teach our horses to stay with us, physically, emotionally and mentally. This is a fun groundwork exercise you can do with your horse to build this connection. It's called the Magic Corner exercise.

Tools: You will need a halter and lead rope for the horse, and you can also use a flag if you wish. A flag is a stick about a metre long, that has a piece of material attached to the end of it.

The setup: If you are in a paddock or field I want you to make a rectangular shape inside it. Maybe just put some barrels or blocks or jump uprights in 4 corners. Wherever you are, just make it obvious to both you and the horse that you can both see a rectangular enclosure. If you're in an arena, then there is no set up required.

Exercise: Walk along the perimeter of your arena or enclosure. As you walk your shoulder will be beside your horse's shoulder. You will be walking closer to the inside of the space, and your horse will be on the outside.

There are four corners in your arena or rectangle. When you turn each corner the horse should stay with you - even if it means they need to walk the straight sides and jog the corners.

The idea is that they figure out their own speed and change their speed when required so that they stay shoulder to shoulder with you. The goal is for all of this to be done on a loose rope. You are working to help the horse be physically, mentally and emotionally with you.

This exercise requires your horse to focus on you, and for you to focus on your horse. It's a great way to ask your horse to do lots of effortless walk to trot to walk transitions. The goal is to be able to take this into your riding. As you both improve your focus and attention on each other this will lead to better transitions, better stops, smaller cues and better communication. Repeat this going both directions.

Dancing with Matilda

I was working on the Magic Corner exercise a few weeks ago with my horse Matilda. We started off shoulder to shoulder at a brisk walk around the perimeter of the arena. For the first corner, she was a little slow, so I used some little vocal encouragement to ask her to gently keep up.

We continued at a nice brisk walk. A step or two away from the next corner Matilda moved into a slow trot, trotted 3 or 4 steps around the corner staying exactly beside me, and then by herself went back to walking again. The lead rope stayed slack (with a smile in the rope) the whole time. It really felt like magic!

We continued on like this for 3 or 4 laps of the arena. The lead rope felt weightless in my hands. Every straight side we would walk together, mirroring each other's steps. Each corner she would do a few steps of trot by herself, and then come back to a walk.

We felt so together and connected to each other. Matilda was following my speed and it was becoming more like a beautiful dance. It was a great way to help Matilda to change gait **without creating any braces or tension in her body.**

Common mistakes to avoid

- Don't pull on the lead rope. If your horse is too slow, you can wave the flag behind the horse gently to encourage them to speed up when needed.
- If your horse isn't relaxed you may need to revisit your comfort zones, or go back to work on confidence issues.
- If your horse is too fast you may be able to slow them down with your voice, or possibly by putting the flag out in front of them.
- If there is an area where your horse is nervous and may jump sideways unexpectedly don't use that location for this exercise - as if your horse spooks they could push into you. Only do this exercise in an area where the horse is comfortable. So if there is a spooky corner in your arena, perhaps just use half the arena for this particular exercise.

Polework exercises

I spent most of today sitting inside, warm and cosy with a cup of tea, catching up on emails at my computer. My horses Ozzie and Matilda were muddy but happy, and were grazing on the hill outside. At about 3.30pm, I looked out the window and decided I had enough work done for the day. I thought:

"I wonder what the horses are doing."

So I pushed back my chair, put my tea cup away and put on my coat to go outside. As I was putting on my wellies I passed where I kept their halters.

What could I do with either Ozzie or Matilda, that would be handy to set up, and take just 10-15 minutes? After working for most of the day, it was all I had time for. Light was starting to fade already, so I had to start doing their feeds a little after 4pm.

I figured out what we would do. We'd do some groundwork with poles! So I grabbed a halter, walked down the paddock and shouted

"OzzzzzzziEEEEEEEEEEEEE!"

The sound of my voice echoed around the parish (something the neighbours are surely used to by now!). About 15 seconds later a very muddy grey Connemara and an even muddier bay mare appeared at the top of the hill.

I walked over, put the halter on Ozzie and decided I would take out three coloured poles and have some fun with them. I really like doing exercises using poles – especially on a day like this when I'm short of time – because you can have a simple pole work exercise set up in less than 20 seconds!

First up we started with the 1 pole challenge. Sometimes Ozzie gets this straight away, and sometimes it takes him a few attempts.

Glossary: The 1 pole challenge is a polework exercise, suitable for all horses. It only requires one pole on the ground. It is simple but it is definitely not easy.

This time he got it perfectly and he looked pretty proud of himself. For fun we did it in the other direction and that was no problem either.

Then I decided to create a triangle out of the poles, and raise up one corner. Oz was taking great interest in what I was doing. He loves nothing more than walking around and demolishing any type of jump or pole structure I assemble!

So we played a little with the triangle. We went over it in different directions. We went over it in a slow and fast walk and then in a trot. It was really nice to be able to spend some time with Ozzie and have fun together. I noticed that it was after 4pm, so we ended it there. I said thanks to Ozzie, gave Matilda a three minute groom (she adores any time spent in a back scratching or grooming session) and headed back in to sort out their food for the evening.

Polework exercises are great when you don't have a lot of time. You can do so many fun exercises with them on the ground. So they are perfect for a day when you are short on time, or when the weather isn't great.

Tip: "Polework exercises are exercises which involve poles lying on the ground. The poles are often made from wood or plastic, and are usually about 10 to 12 feet long. The diameter is approximately 4 inches. Poles can be bought in local tack shops, or wooden poles (which can be painted various colours) can be found at local hardware stores."

6 Benefits of polework exercises

I love using lots of different polework layouts with my horses to keep our time together fun and interesting. There are so many different ways you can arrange poles, and you can use them for both groundwork and riding obstacles. You can ask your horse to walk, trot or canter over them, and you can use them to improve your transitions as well.

Meet one of our students, Nancy Thompson-Perkins, owner of Wyndym Equine at Mulgrave, Canada.

"I adopt and re-train standardbred race horses… Standardbred horses never really see the need to pick up their feet. It's not something they are trained to do in their racing careers. So when they come to me, most of the time they just need some biomechanics training. And picking up their legs and feet over a pole is great to condition them into riding horses.

When we first started all I could hear was the clunking of their hooves hitting the poles. But then their core started to engage and they were picking their legs up higher. The bend in their bodies was so relaxing for them. Listening to the relaxed sighs and exhales of breath was the biggest change that I enjoyed the most.

The core of the horse was being exercised and their minds were kept busy with different pole exercises which relaxed their bodies and minds. It was a Win-Win situation."

I love doing pole work with my horses for many reasons, including:

- Helping improve my horse's precision, agility and focus.
- Helping improve my horses flexibility, core strength, balance and straightness.
- My horses LOVE them! And If my horse is happy, I am happy too.
- You can be so creative with how you set them up, the options are endless.
- They are a lot of fun.
- You can get started with just one or two poles. So they are very inexpensive to set up.

"I needed some exercises that would help my horse become more relaxed, more balanced, and more trusting. Doing polework exercises have helped my horse to become more relaxed and more balanced. The pole work has also helped him to learn to slow down and "think." This is important because his solution to many problems was to rush through puzzles and obstacles. The pole work has also taught him "where his feet are," which is important when we're out on the trails navigating trappy footing. The biggest "win" for me and my horse is more trust between us. More trust means more willingness and less anxiety." Heidi, USA.

Polework challenges are fun groundwork exercises where the goal is often to just stand still in a certain position.

The one pole challenge is probably the best known of these. It is super for bad weather or when the ground is hard and it is not safe to go faster than a walk. It is a great exercise if you only have 15 mins to do something with your horse. It is perfect to do in the winter.

Setup:

Put 1 pole on the ground. The goal is to ask your horse to place their off fore and off hind on one side of the pole and to place their near fore and near hind on the other side of the pole. It sounds simple, but it's not easy!

Glossary: *The near side of the horse is the left side, which is the side most people mount and dismount from. The off side of your horse is the right side.*

The one pole exercise can take a number of days to complete. I would work on this for no longer than five minutes at a time. I would 'eat the elephant' and break it down into a lot of tiny steps. The first goal might be to ask your horse to step over the pole with one front foot and to stand still there.

There is no one correct method to do this exercise. You can begin by walking the horse towards the pole, or having your horse stand in any position near the pole. The idea is that you choose your approach by trying to figure out what would be the easiest thing for your horse to accomplish. This is tricky for some people, who like to follow instructions and are not used to being 'creative' and are worried about getting things 'wrong'.

There is no wrong move in this exercise. This is a great exercise to help very process-oriented people to experience and explore their creative side more. This is very important as our horses need us to be creative - sometimes way more creative than we are in our normal lives.

I love this exercise because it's wonderful for horses:

- It improves the horse's proprioception, and their awareness of where their feet are.
- It requires the horse to really focus and figure out what you're asking for.
- It allows the horse to have a series of 'tiny wins' and to be praised often, which builds confidence in the horse.
- It improves communication between horse and human.
- It helps the horse to understand the cues to ask just one foot to step sideways (useful for lateral work in the future!).
- It's a lot more interesting for the horse than never-ending circles.
- It helps you and your horse feel like a team together.

I love this exercise because it's wonderful for humans:

- No more aimlessly wandering around the arena, not sure what to do next.
- The human has a clear purpose and a goal.
- The human has to learn to use tiny cues. If the cues are too big, you can't complete the challenge.
- The human has to read the horse's body language and start to predict any balance changes in the horse. So our awareness level improves. This helps every aspect of our horsemanship.
- The human has to become more patient.

- It teaches the human to break down one complicated task into a lot of tiny tasks which are much easier to achieve.
- It teaches the human to slow down and enjoy the journey and the small improvements, instead of trying to get things done super fast.

When I did it for the first time with my two horses Ozzie, my Connemara, figured it out in a few minutes on day one, but most horses will not do this. It took my other horse, Matilda, three days to figure it out. Many of my students have taken up to a week or more. The time it takes is not important. The process of doing the exercise is what is important.

Useful tip: Before you begin, set a generous expectation for this challenge. Assume your horse will take 7 short sessions (over at least 7 days) to figure this out. This doesn't need to be 7 days in a row. It is simply the next 7 times you spend time with your horse.

Each day you're hoping for a tiny improvement.

- Day 1 might be standing beside the pole.
- Day 2 might be 1 front foot over.
- Day 3 might be 2 front feet over, but the hind feet get stuck.

And so on.

The key is to use tiny cues and break this one challenge down into tiny steps. Then reward the horse with a rest and words of praise each time they get a tiny piece of the puzzle figured out.

The goal is not speed. The goal is to build your skills as a horseman or horsewoman, by using this exercise and by listening to the horse in the process. Because this exercise is all about communication, patience and timing it's a super way to build trust and partnership with your horse.

"Today I decided not to ride as there were lots of walkers about. I decided to work on the one pole challenge instead and we managed to do it! My horse Skye was a bit confused at first, and was really thinking about where she was placing her feet. She's becoming really responsive to slight pressure to ask her to move her shoulders and hindquarters." Emma, UK.

The 1 pole challenge exercise

Complete the 1 pole challenge with your horse. Be patient as it may take 7 days or more.

Cavaletti

Cavaletti exercises are similar to polework exercises. You use the same poles but instead of the poles lying on the ground, one or both ends of the poles are raised up a few inches off the ground. The idea is not that the horse jumps them - but the horse picks up his feet a little higher when he goes over them. They are a lot of fun.

You can do cavaletti exercises both on the ground and also when riding your horse. They are another great way to add fun and creativity into your time with your horse.

Cavaletti exercise

Set up 3 cavaletti and ask your horse to walk over them.

Sideways exercises

When you start riding a new or young horse you start with the basics. Things like helping your horse to be confident, and teaching them to go forwards and backwards. You are looking to help your horse respond when you ask them to turn right or left. These are the very basics we need in place with all riding horses.

Once you have forwards, backwards and turning right and left in place, you've got the basics mastered. The next step is to teach your horse to go sideways.

All horses, including quarter horses, thoroughbreds, arabs, paints, cobs, Tennessee walking horses, connemaras, trail riding horses, jumping horses and more, will see improvements in their balance and posture when they begin to add in some sideways movements to their training.

One common misconception is that to ask your horse to do any type of sideways movement, you need a dressage horse. This is completely untrue. Your horse does not need to be a dressage horse.

You do not even need a dressage arena to teach your horse some simple sideways movements. In fact, you can do this on trail rides, along a fence line, on the ground - anywhere you want. Sideways exercises are great for all riding horses, no matter what discipline you enjoy or the breed of your horse.

Another term to describe asking a horse to go sideways, is 'lateral work'.

Lateral work

'Lateral work is another way to describe any type of exercise that requires the horse to do some form of sideways movement.'

Lateral work is very important for the horse for a number of reasons.

When we sit on a horse to ride them we change the horse's balance and posture. By nature horses already have the majority of their weight on the forehand - on their front two legs. When we ride them our additional weight puts even more weight on their forehand. Even just by us sitting in the saddle, their withers (the area just in front of the saddle, near where the mane starts) will drop a little. With this extra weight on the horse's two front legs, what tends to happen is that their backs hollow, and often their heads will be quite high as a result. When you ride them they can look a little like they are plodding along, or dragging themselves forwards with their front feet.

This way of carrying the rider's weight will put all types of stresses and strains on our horses' bodies. Logically, horses weren't designed to have a human on their back. So when we ride them they have all this extra weight added on their front legs. If the horse is allowed to use this type of posture over months and years it can lead to serious health issues like kissing spines, back issues, early retirement, joint problems, feet issues and more.

It's similar to us picking up a heavy box without bending our knees. We can do it a few times and be ok. However at some stage it's quite likely that we will pull something in our back, or cause some type of strain.

Back issues can be both very painful, debilitating and very difficult and expensive to fix. If your horse has a sore back, you can't ride them!

So in order to keep their bodies healthy when we ride them, and to make it physically as easy as possible for them to carry us, we need to do a few things. We need to figure out what exercises we can teach our riding horses that will encourage them to transfer some of the weight from their forequarters to their hindquarters. This will change our horse's balance and posture. By doing this we greatly reduce the potential for any back issues when we are riding our horses.

The technical term for the result - the transfer of weight from the forelegs to the hindlegs - is called *collection*. Collection is about a shift of balance, not a head position as many riders seem to think.

Collection

When we help the horse to transfer some weight from his two front legs to his two hindlegs, a few things happen that are really good for our horse's health. The first is that collection becomes possible. True collection isn't a head position. For true collection to happen there needs to be a shift of the weight from the front end to the hindquarters. When that happens the horse will be able to carry us in a way that is balanced and athletic. The door to "self carriage" (when the horse carries themselves without the rider needing to hold them) opens.

- The horse's hindquarters are designed to carry weight. There are a lot more bendy pieces in the hind legs, than in the front legs. So we are setting them up to be able to carry themselves in a better way.
- When the horse's balance shifts more to the hindquarters their back stops hollowing out, making it easier to carry a rider's weight with less potential to cause back issues. As many of us spend hundreds - if not thousands - of hours in the saddle each year, this is really important to teach our horses.
- When we teach our horses collection it helps them to become more athletic and physically powerful. If you look at any of the old paintings of people riding horses in war, they have a lot of weight on their hindquarters, their backs are rounded, their neck and head position is a natural result of the weight on their hindquarters - and not created by riders pulling on their reins. Quite often in those old pictures the reins actually have slack in them! During these times the horse was the ultimate athlete - ready to jump, gallop and go sideways at a split second's notice, to avoid death on the battlefield and to stay safe from the enemy.

How do we start collection?

This all sounds good. I hope we all believe that horses should be treated kindly, and trained and ridden in a way that protects their long-term health. In practical terms, trying to teach your horse various exercises that result in 'collection' might sound like something that could be really complicated to try and do.

This truth is - it's actually very doable! Meet Doris, from the USA.

"It wasn't just the shoulder out training that helped us. I had taken a fall off my horse when he spooked at a puddle of light. I am 67. I do NOT bounce..I lost my confidence, but wanted to find a way to interact with my boy and regain my confidence while not jeopardizing myself physically. I actually began feeling like a horse trainer. I think that was the biggest change - that I felt I was actually teaching my horse something." Doris, Canada.

I promise both you and your horse will be able to do it. I promise that it works great for all breeds including **quarter horses, thoroughbreds, arabs, paints, cobs, tennessee walking horses, connemaras, trail riding horses, jumping horses** - all of them. It also works for both Western and English riders. All you need is a horse over three years of age and a willingness to try it out!

"My name is Mary. I am from Cornwall UK and my horse is Mr Valentine, he is an 18 year old Arab gelding. I felt we were not connected under saddle. The conventional way to hold the reins (to my mind) set up a fight with him, so neither of us is relaxed. I was hoping this training will help soften us both to collect in a relaxed way. We have begun very slowly starting with just walking in a

straight line shoulder to shoulder as he likes to follow. A few steps of shoulder out have been achieved on the right rein, on three tracks. Left rein is more tricky as he tends to be stiffer so have taken it slowly. Noted that my position (head up) is critical to keep him moving forward. The long lead rope has really helped. We are now able to do shoulder out on both reins which is great. Only a few steps on the stiffer side but I am so pleased we are much better connected and relaxed. It's a great way to connect with your horse to find balance and collection in a gentle relaxed way." Mary, UK.

Hello Dressage

You've probably seen dressage competitions on the TV. In dressage, there can be a lot of 'fancy' and what look like complicated moves. You've probably heard of a few of them; half pass, hindquarters out, shoulder in, piaffe, passage and others. Many of the movements that dressage horses are doing actually originate from the battlefields many centuries ago.

In the battlefield horses needed to be collected and light and to be able to quickly stop, go, turn, canter sideways, move their hindquarters, move their forequarters and intimidate their enemy. The groundwork and riding exercises the riders did helped their horses to transfer their weight to their hindquarters, get lighter and softer and become awesome high level performance athletes.

Many of these old style dressage exercises are fantastic ways to help your horse to carry a rider, carry more weight on his hindquarters and improve his posture - and in doing so help to protect the health of his back.

Why does lateral work help collection?

So how do you teach yourself and your horse how to begin collection? The answer is very simple.

I want to share with you the first two exercises I recommend you teach your horse, which includes asking one hind leg at a time to steep a little deeper underneath the horse's body. When we ask just one hind leg to step a little deeper underneath the horse's body, it transfers some of the horse's weight from their forequarters to their hindquarters. This changes the horse's balance and improves their posture.

These two exercises are called shoulder in and shoulder out.

- You can do these exercises on the ground, and you can do them when you are riding.
- You can start to teach them to your horse in just five minutes!
- Any horse over 3 years of age can be taught to do shoulder in and out.

"These exercises are like going to the gym for your horse and they also help with connection, as you are using small cues to communicate." Karen, England.

Glossary: shoulder in and shoulder out

Shoulder in is a movement that we can ask the horse to perform both on the ground and when we are riding them. It involves asking the horse to move both forwards and sideways at the same time, with a specific posture. Shoulder out is the mirror image of shoulder in.

Shoulder in and out are super for many reasons:

- Improving the horse's balance.
- Encouraging the horse to transfer weight from forequarters to hindquarters.
- Helping the horse become more athletic.
- Improving the horse's physical posture.
- Beginning to work in collection (the most healthy way for a horse to carry the weight of a rider).
- Helping the horse to be able to move and turn with more agility and flexibility.
- When you ride your horse will feel lighter and more responsive to smaller cues.
- They are the first two exercises you need to begin teaching your horse lateral movements - which you can use later in western riding, cow work and dressage.
- Any horse can do this!
- You can start teaching this with a simple 5 minute exercise on the ground.

Our students have seen the results too.

"Shoulder in and out has helped my horse to understand she can go sideways as well as forwards. Our relationship has improved as has her confidence in me." Rachel, UK

First it's useful to have a picture of what the exercises should look like. Imagine the green top of the banana in this illustration is your horse's head.

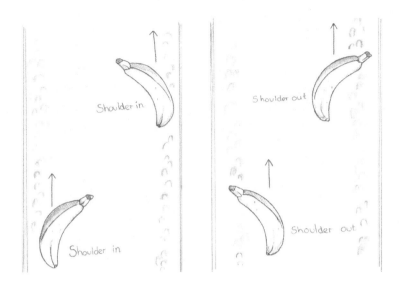

During shoulder out there is a gentle bend going through the horse's whole body. The horse's head, neck and shoulders are close to the fence line and their hindquarters are a little more towards the inside of the arena.

Shoulder in is the exact same movement, just with the horse looking into the arena with their hindquarters closer to the outside of the arena.

Here is another way to look at it. Normally when you ride a horse if you were to look at its hoofprints in the sand you would see two lines of hoofprints. With shoulder out, you can see either 3 lines of hoofprints (3 track shoulder in) or 4 lines of hoofprints (4 track shoulder in).

Imagine you have a fence line in your paddock. You would like to ask your horse to walk along that fence line, with shoulders near the fence line, and their hindquarters a little further away from the fenceline. So the horse's shoulders are pointing slightly towards the fenceline, and their hindquarters are a little away from the fenceline.

There is a gentle bend throughout the whole body of the horse. This is shoulder out. Your goal is to see three tracks of hoofprints along the fence line. This is 3 track shoulder out.

If you repeat this exercise, but ask the horse to increase the bend through their body a little, the angle of their body compared to the fence will change. You will notice that your horse is leaving 4 tracks of hoofprints along the fence line. This is 4 track shoulder out.

How to start shoulder out

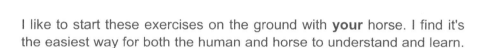

I like to start these exercises on the ground with **your** horse. I find it's the easiest way for both the human and horse to understand and learn. There are a few things to bear in mind

- The whole horse's body has a gentle bend through it.
- The horse's head is closer to the outside of the arena.
- The horse's hindquarters are closer to the inside of the arena.
- When a horse walks normally towards you his legs are on two tracks, his hind feet generally follow the direction of the front feet. When doing shoulder out your horse's feet will be on three or even four tracks, depending on how much bend is in his body. Both of these are useful for different training purposes.

Equipment and setup:

- A fenceline.
- A halter or headcollar.
- A lead rope that is at least 12 ft in length (a short lead rope won't work).

- If you have nothing else you can try with a longer lunge line or a 22ft line, but carrying a longer rope like this can be a bit difficult to handle.
- A horse who is happy with your patting and rubbing their hindquarters. If your horse gets worried when someone is near their hindquarters, or is very spooky, nervous or kicks, you are not ready to do this exercise. Instead you need to go back to basics to build confidence and relaxation instead.

Instructions:

- Walk along the fence line with your horse in hand.
- You are between your horse and the fence.
- Allow the lead rope to get longer and your horse to walk slightly ahead of you.
- Walk a little more towards their ribs to ask the hindquarters to move away from the fence line.
- All you want is a step or two to begin with, then walk on forwards normally again.
- Praise your horse and tell them they are wonderful!

The Shoulder out exercise

Try one step of shoulder out on the ground with your horse

Young, older and new horses

Having a young horse is the most amazing opportunity. You get them to teach them everything they need to be happy and confident around humans and to train them right from the beginning in a way that protects their long-term health.

I believe in not starting horses until they are at least 4 or 5 years of age. It's only at a minimum of 5.5 years of age that a horse's back may be fully mature. If you do a lot of riding work before that age... well - there are a lot of ways you can damage your horse's body.

I started my young horse Matilda at five years of age and everything I did was with the goal to keep her happy and healthy for many years to come. When I started to work with her I didn't just get her used to a saddle and bridle and then jump on her back. I actually spent a few months doing groundwork, and preparing her mind and body for the future.

One of the first groundwork exercises I did with her, after I was happy she could lead and stop and turn lightly, was the shoulder out. It is a wonderful introduction to helping horses move their weight more to their hindquarters, it's also great to establish your personal space as they have to yield away from you. On top of all that you get to spend valuable time building a really good relationship with your horse. It makes sense right? If you want to start riding a young horse, I think it's a wonderful idea, before you ride, to teach them how to carry your weight in the saddle. You can do this really easily with young horses, by doing this simple shoulder out exercise on the ground.

I recommend shoulder out on the ground (and shoulder in when you get further) as a great exercise for all young horses before they are ridden.

Older and retired horses

When I own a horse I commit to having that horse for their full lifetime. I don't believe in passing on older horses when they can't be ridden any more, or selling them when you decide to buy a more exciting young horse.

For me, horses are for life. They are not for throwing away.

Of course, older horses have different physical needs. Some may struggle to put on as much condition as they did when they were younger. Some may not be in regular training with you any more and live most of their lives out in the pasture. Some may have lost significant muscle tone along their back and topline. When you ask a horse to do a shoulder out or in, by asking their whole body to bend you are working on building those topline muscles which may be lacking in the older horse. So this little groundwork exercise can actually benefit your older horse's health.

Meet Debbi from Southern California.

"Shoulder in & out are exercises I wish I had had 11 yrs ago. But I guess the teacher arrives when the student is ready. I have a 22 year old Friesian gelding. He has always been swaybacked and was always heavy on my hands. He used his front end but not so much his hindquarters.

Elaine's shoulder out training has helped our already great relationship. I watched your videos many times. The shoulder out on the ground is a great way for us to be 'present' with each other. The win here is our relationship. I am 'present' and he is patient and kind - and doing the work as well! Four and three track shoulder out, and not only in the arena but we also practice on trails. It is always a win-win when I 'get it' I get all giddy like a schoolgirl (I am 64 and we have been together 11 yrs!) when we are in sync and doing the exercise correctly! Your bite size pieces for this exercise were fundamental in my learning process. I loved it, and so does my horse." Deb, USA.

The funny thing about teaching horses things... is that when we repeat things, habits start to form. I have seen horses who have been introduced to lateral work, and taught how to transfer their weight from their forequarters to their hindquarters, actually start to carry themselves a little differently when free out in the field! It's pretty amazing to see.

If you have a horse who you no longer ride, or you have an older horse, this exercise is a wonderful way to spend time with your horse while improving their long term health.

5 Common mistakes to avoid about collection

Collection is often misunderstood in the horse world. Here are 5 common mistakes and beliefs to avoid.

"To teach collection you must first use the reins to get your horse's nose to be vertical."

This is completely **FALSE**. Collection is based on the transferring of weight from the horses forequarters to the hindquarters. This is done by showing the horse how to step his hind legs deeper underneath himself through lateral work. Pulling a horse's head in is 1) painful for the horse 2) eliminates the potential for any lightness or softness to develop 3) makes collection impossible as a horse physically cannot move his weight to his hindquarters if his nose is behind the vertical.

"To be collected the poll must be below withers."

FALSE. Any horse with the poll below the withers is not collected. It is physically impossible as there is too much weight dumped on the forehand. Yes I know this is the 'fashion' in some western riding today but it is not good for your horse's long term health.

"If I use gadgets like side reins and other (nefarious!) training devices, they will teach my horse collection".

FALSE. There are no gadgets that will replace good horsemanship. Most of these gadgets are uncomfortable at least and abusive at the worst. Using gadgets ignores the fact that if you teach the horse's mind it's easy to train the body with good posture habits, through patience and understanding. There is no value in compliance achieved through pain.

"I'm not good enough to do this".

FALSE. A common problem with collection and lateral work is that sometimes it's explained in a way that is very difficult to understand. In fact, it's not that complicated, once you understand the step by step process and how to get started.

Imagine what life would feel like when your horse is doing shoulder out. The weight transfer to the hindquarters is beginning and your horse is improving his health. Your horse is not as heavy to ride as usual. Softness and lightness are starting to develop throughout your horsemanship.

It would be pretty cool, right? :)

This is not rocket science. You can do it! Regardless of your age or experience level. You now have the knowledge, the skills and the desire to try.

"My horse is too old to learn new things."

FALSE. Your horse is very smart. I'd say that horses actually learn things faster than we do.

Have you ever tried to change a habit, for example, like not looking down when you ride? It can take forever! But have you ever seen how much a horse can change in just a few minutes with a great rider or trainer? :) Your horse has the potential to learn lots of new things, regardless of their age or breed.

You can do it - and your horse can do it too.

Homework: Share one common belief you have heard about collection that is not true.

Riding

The Royal Stables in Cordoba, Spain

I got an email one evening about two years ago. It was about an upcoming film trip I had planned to Spain that April.

"Elaine, we are all set for filming in Spain. But I had one question. Do you want to get a private garrocha lesson at the Royal Stables when you are here?"

Side note: A garrocha is a type of long wooden pole that is traditionally used in Spain to herd bulls. Riding with a garrocha is a very effective way for riders to improve their balance and posture in the saddle. For training purposes lighter options, such as fibreglass poles, can be used.

My heart was doing 90 miles an hour. I had literally stopped breathing. The Royal Stables in Cordoba, Spain is home to the Andalusian horse and renowned throughout Europe and the world.

I had just been invited to get a 1-1 lesson, at the Royal Stables, on a Spanish horse!

"A private garrocha lesson, wow!" I managed to reply. I knew that normally you cannot book this type of lesson and that it was a great honor to be asked.

"Yes. We can arrange it for the Friday that you are here. Just think about it and let me know if you want to arrange it."

"Sounds great. Let me double check and I'll get back to you tomorrow."

Now here is the honest truth. I felt out of my depth.

I had a big issue. I had an annoying voice inside me asking: 'Are you sure about this?' Because the truth was I didn't think I was worthy, or good enough, to ride at the Royal Stables in Cordoba.

Sure, I'd ridden with a garrocha before and Ozzie loves it when I take it out. But riding my own horse, who I adore, by myself with no pressure in Ireland - is a lot different to packing my bags, flying to Spain, and getting a private 1-1 lesson at the birthplace of the Andalusian horses at the Royal Stables!

- What if I didn't ride well?
- What if I dropped the garrocha?
- What if I spent the hour just confusing both the horse and the instructor?!

The problem was that a small part of me didn't think I was good enough to ride at the Royal Stables.

So I thought about it, and decided to ring a friend whose opinion I value a lot.

"Hey, it's Elaine. Can I get your advice on something?"
"Sure, whats up?"
"I've got an opportunity to get a 1-1 garrocha lesson at the Royal Stables in Cordoba. I know it'd be an amazing opportunity, but I'm not sure if I should ride."

There was a pause at the end of the line. After a few moments, the response came back.

"I don't see why not."

There was another pause on the line. My friend was 110% correct. There was no valid reason why I needed to pass up the opportunity of a lifetime.

So I made my decision. The next day I confirmed my garrocha lesson at the Royal Stables in Cordoba. I realised that having the opportunity to ride a beautifully trained Spanish horse, under the careful watch of a super talented Spanish garrocha instructor at the Royal Stables in Cordoba, would help me so much with my own horses and greatly expand my riding knowledge and skills.

It was time to say goodbye to my comfort zone. So I packed my bags, jumped on the plane and headed with my riding gear to Andalucia.

On Friday I walked up to the magnificent wooden doors of the Royal Stables. I was both nervous and excited. I met my instructor, who was really nice, and I had a gorgeous 16hh Spanish horse to meet as well!

For the first 30 minutes we worked on circles, shoulder out, shoulder in, leg yields and half pass in walk. Then we repeated everything in the canter. We worked on some walk to canter departs. We did very little work in trot. It was generally - try it in walk, then repeat it in the canter.

My horse was ridden in a totally different style to what I was used to. It was up to me to learn quickly so I could use similar cues to the riders who usually ride this horse.

Half way through the lesson it was time to pick up the garrocha. I was so excited! My instructor taught me a series of five movements with the garrocha. The first step was to memorise these and then do them in walk with my horse. At this stage as I was holding the garrocha I was also riding one handed.

That went great.

'OK, now we do them in canter'".

Right. I took a deep breath and did a quick run through the aids for a walk to canter depart and got ready. Riding one handed, off I went. We did a lovely walk to canter transition and as we cantered around in a small circle, I performed the sequence of garrocha movements successfully.

OMG I was so thrilled!!

I had finally ridden a garrocha sequence, in canter, on a Spanish horse, at the Royal Stables in Cordoba and it actually was quite good!

I was on cloud nine. And that's when it happened.

My instructor looked and me and he said,

'Very good. Now the other direction in canter'.

I took a moment to figure out in my head what the garrocha pattern would be going anti-clockwise. Because here is the thing you might not know about the garrocha. When you do clockwise circles, holding a garrocha is quite straightforward. The garrocha (the very long wooden pole) is held in your right hand. When you're going clockwise it's easy to let the end of the garrocha rest on the ground, in the middle of the circle.

But here is the issue. When you are riding anti-clockwise circles, the garrocha is still held in your right hand. So if you want to rest the end of the garrocha in the middle of the anti-clockwise circle, you need to first raise the garrocha up high and lift the entire garrocha over you and your horse's body.

Going anti-clockwise with a traditional Spanish garrocha (the end of a traditionally made Spanish garrocha is very sharp!) is really tricky.

As I sat in the saddle, under the midday Spanish sun, I realised the challenge I was about to face. I started to doubt my abilities. I didn't think I could do it.

My instructor could see my indecision written all over my face. And he took one look at me and said:

"If not now - then when?"

Honestly, he had a very good point.

I was sitting on a very well trained Spanish horse, at the Royal Stables, with a great instructor to help me. In fact, there would literally be no better time in the world to try this! So I gave a big smile and I said "OK"!

I took a deep breath, gathered up the reins in my left hand and executed a walk to canter depart, moving on an anti-clockwise circle. After a few strides I thought, 'it's now or never' and I executed the garrocha sequence to the left perfectly.

I floated the whole way back home after that lesson!

But here is the thing.

It's normal to have that little voice inside you that says '*you're not good enough'.*

But it's not actually true. We all have the ability to achieve a lot more than we ever thought was possible.

My horses, Ozzie and Matilda, deserve me to do everything in my power that I can, to become the best rider possible. I am going to do everything I can to develop my skills for them.

I think you should do that for your horses too. We should never limit our dreams.

Spanish, English, Western, German or Californian?

As a horsewomen, I am happy to be a little unusual. I'm an Irish rider, who rides with a German made Baroque saddle, a California hackamore and I have been known to fly to Spain and Australia for riding lessons.

However, the truth is that I want to do all I can to become a better rider and horsewoman. Before we move on to the riding exercises I love doing with my horses, let's look at the tools we have available to us, across the range of riding styles.

Riding tools - The bit and bridle

The equipment that we use with our horses when we ride is critically important. The most common type of bridle I see usually has a bit of some sort. Discussing bits would require an entire book just by itself. However I just wanted to include some important points to bear in mind if you are using a bit with your horse.

- A horse's mouth is very delicate. If you are rough or fast with your hands, or use your hands to balance yourself when you ride, this is a great way to damage your horse's mouth.
- There are certain traditions (such as the California hackamore tradition) who only put a bit into the horse's mouth after that horse has already been fully trained without a bit. The reason to do this is to protect the health of the horse's mouth.
- The anatomy of each horse's mouth is different. Some horses have a lot of room for a bit. Some horse's mouths have barely any room for a bit. It would be worthwhile to ask your dentist - who sees the anatomy of many horses' mouths daily as part of their work - to tell you what mouth anatomy your horse has, and what type of bits to avoid. Some of you will be able to access a consultation from an experienced bit fitter, which is well worth doing.
- When you purchase a horse you might also get their bridle. Do not assume that the bit that comes with the horse will actually fit the horse correctly.
- Inside the horse's mouth are a lot of teeth. The anatomy of some horse's mouths, mean that where the bit would naturally lie, is where a tooth is growing. So if you put a bit into that horse's mouth, when the bit hits the tooth it will cause extreme pain. In cases like this, using a bridle without a bit would be worth looking into.

- You always want to be aware of any damage occurring inside your horse's mouth. One way to check is to ask your dentist during each visit whether there is any scarring or ulcers present in your horse's mouth. If yes, these are all red flags and you will need to investigate the cause. You can also check your horse's mouth yourself. Damage and bruising are quite easy to see.
- If your horse has pain in his mouth, caused by anything from a loose tooth, to an ulcer, to a bit pinching the tongue, the horse has no simple way to alert us to this issue. The horse may suffer in silence for months or years (awful), or the horse may try to avoid the pain, by raising its head up, opening its mouth a lot, trying to go too fast when we ride, rearing, bucking, bolting, trying to avoid the bit or not wanting to be bridled. These are all signs we need to investigate.
- Bridles also need to fit. In particular they should not be too tight over the brow or around the ears as this can cause a lot of discomfort.

We cannot hope to develop a happy riding horse if the bit in our horse's mouth is causing the horse pain.

"When I went to try out Jasper it was quite an interesting experience. His owners let me ride him out alone and it was clear that he was the perfect hacking horse. He was so relaxed and confident. However he kept pushing down with his head and opening his mouth. I decided he wasn't happy with something and just gave him plenty of rein, which seemed to help. I put a deposit down subject to vetting.

The vet found that Jasper had a very sore mouth. He had sharp teeth which had caused ulcers. He must have been in a lot of pain and yet was kind enough to allow people to carry on riding him - what horses put up with from us! He came home to me and had dental treatment done under sedation. After a little break for his mouth to heal I started riding him and he was great, all the leaning and opening his mouth had gone." Sue, UK.

One significant issue with bits today is that we have lost the art of fitting them. Certainly in some parts of the US, people used to have full time jobs travelling around fitting bits all day. It can be difficult to find this type of person, with years of month anatomy and bit fitting experience, today although happily that is changing in some parts of the world.

As a result it's not hard to imagine that most bits are not chosen based on the horse's individual mouth confirmation, but because it was recommend as a 'kind bit' in a tack shop, or as a 'good bit' by a friend who uses it on their horse (who likely has a totally different mouth anatomy), or is a favourite on a social media group.

Bitless bridles

Throughout the world of horsemanship there is increasing interest in the use of bitless bridles. People have different reasons for wanting to find out more about riding bitless. Some because their horses are clearly uncomfortable being ridden with a bit. Others are convinced that bits are physically harmful to horses and that bitless is a safer option. Some riders just want to try something different.

I wanted to find out more about how people felt about bitless bridles, what their concerns were and what they needed to know, so I conducted a survey in our community. The results of the survey were fascinating.

It showed that many horse owners were keen to learn more about riding without a bit. Of those surveyed:

- 78% said that they would like to try bitless
- 15% said that they might try bitless
- 6% said that they would not try bitless

Are horses really happier in bitless bridles?

It's certainly an interesting question. For some horses, who have the perfectly fitted bit, and a rider with kind and sensitive hands, they may be equally comfortable in both.

Some horses dislike particular types of bitless bridles. For example, some don't like the restriction of cross under bridles, or the poll pressure on mechanical hackamores. So you could argue they would also prefer a bit.

96.2% of all bitless riders surveyed in our community said their horse was happier in a bitless bridle, compared to a bit.

Which bitless bridle is right for my horse?

In general, bitless bridles fall into one of the following 5 categories:

- Rope halters and headcollars
- Sidepulls
- Mechanical hackamores
- Cross-under
- Hackamores

Bitless bridles are no different to any other in that they should fit your horse properly, no one size fits all. Your horse should have plenty of room around their ears and over their forehead so that they aren't feeling pinched by the bridle. The noseband should always be positioned on the nasal bone, above the delicate pointed area at the end of the bone and the nose cavity.

Sometimes riders are advised to lower the noseband on a bitless bridle to give more control, I would not support that in any situation as it can cause pain and injury. In a similar way, I do not recommend any bitless bridle that straps the horse's mouth shut, or restricts the natural movement of their head and mouth.

Bitless bridles are often made of leather, but also in a variety of materials such as nylon webbing, rope and neoprene, sometimes a combination of things.

Bitless bridle options

Let's look at the different styles used for bitless riding, their action on the horse and give some examples.

Rope halter and headcollar

Rope halters are very popular with bitless riders. They are simple, knotted halters that can be used for ridden work. This will be with the lead rope knotted to make reins, with clip on reins, or with a longer rope tied as a mecate so that there is enough to use as a lead rope while the reins are tied. The fit of rope halters varies widely. My recommendation for a riding halter is that it must be well fitted. Rope halters aren't the most precise tool to ride in as they can move around quite a lot, but if they are properly fitted the aids will make more sense to your horse. The throat piece should sit behind the horse's cheek, rather than on it. The nose band should sit comfortably above the end of the nasal bone. The nose band should also fit quite closely under the jaw without restricting how the horse moves their face. Long, baggy nosebands and fiador knots will affect the action of the halter, so that it acts on the horse's neck rather than its nose. I recommend using a rope without a clip, so that the clip isn't swinging around when you are going above a walk.

There is safety consideration when you use a rope halter, and that is that they will not break. This could be an argument for using clip-on reins that will break at the clip if your horse gets caught up. The clips will be smaller and lighter than lead rope clips, so they shouldn't hit the horse on the jaw. It's certainly a good reason to make sure that the halter fits properly, so that a horse that manages to sneak an itch of its head doesn't run the risk of catching a hoof or shoe in the halter. When you're riding in a rope halter never let your horse put their head down so that they could get a front hoof caught. If you use a mecate length rope, consider what you do with it and how long the loop in the lead rope is when you're in the saddle. Never put a horse into a horse trailer wearing a rope halter as it is a safety risk if something goes wrong.

Some rope halters have rings attached by the knots at the side of the noseband where you can attach reins. Similarly, it's possible to attach reins to the sides of most headcollars. If you do that then you will be riding using a sidepull action.

A friend brought her new pony to a clinic I was attending. She showed everyone the tack that the pony had been wearing when she tried him out. He wore a complicated bridle that strapped his mouth shut, a bit that was designed to stop him leaning and a martingale to keep his head down. We looked at a video of her riding him at the dealers and he looked stressed but also very strong. He was leaning on her hands and looked like he would take off at any minute!

The group spent their morning session working on groundwork with their horses wearing rope halters. They made sure that their horses were flexible in their necks, willing to step their hind legs under and were generally soft and responsive to the halter. That afternoon my friend knotted her halter lead rope into reins, took a deep breath and got on her pony. After a few simple checks to make sure he was responding to her cues they were off! They were able to walk, trot and canter safely and the pony did everything asked of him. It was a very different picture to the video we'd seen. Given nothing to fight against and make him uncomfortable this pony was able to show what a truly safe and responsive partner he could be.

Pros:

- Instant release
- Doesn't tighten on your horse's face
- Useful also for groundwork

Cons:

- Lacks stability on the horse's face so signals can be inconsistent
- The need to be aware that no part of the halter or rope has a break point

Sidepull

The sidepull bridle is a very simple version of a bitless bridle. Often it looks rather like a conventional bridle, but without the attachment for a bit. Your reins are attached at the side of the noseband and therefore give a very clear signal to your horse of the direction in which you want them to turn their head. There will be a very slight pressure on the opposite side of their face from the noseband. There are a lot of un-branded sidepulls available, often from western tack suppliers. Branded options are also available. There are also some light and simple cavesson halters that are designed to be used for riding as well as groundwork. Some sidepull bridles have two additional rings fitted lower down on the noseband that allow the rider to attach a second set of reins. This would give you some poll pressure and could be described as the bitless equivalent of a double bridle.

"When I was riding with a bit, my horse Choupette was always dropping her shoulder to the inside of the circle on the right hand. Whatever I was trying to do, it never really worked. When I used a side pull for the first time the problem disappeared instantly. She automatically became more balanced and was able to bend on the circle. Obviously, the bit was interfering with her movements, and probably my hands as well in a certain way, but my hands did not change when I rode bitless. My horse felt so much better. She never drops her shoulder since she is being ridden bitless." Madeleine, Canada.

Pros:

- Instant release
- Doesn't use poll pressure.
- Doesn't tighten on your horse's face.
- Voted the second best type of bitless bridle to use for advanced riding goals by the Listening to the Horse community.

Cons:

- Some designs can either move on the horse's face, or be quite tight or even too tight.
- Not used much for groundwork (unless cavesson style).
- Cavessons with a metal core should be avoided as they can be harsh.

Cross-under and cross-over

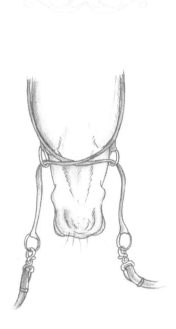

There are two main styles of cross-under bridle. The basic cross-under will either have an extended noseband or a noseband that ends on the side of the horse's face with two straps attached to lengthen it. These straps then cross under your horse's jaw and attach to the reins. This means that cross-under bridles give your horse a different feeling to a sidepull in that they close on the jaw and the direction of feel comes more from underneath the jaw, your horse will also feel some side pressure from the noseband.

The second style of cross-under has an extended head and cheek piece that passes through rings on the noseband, crosses under your horse's jaw and attaches to the reins. So this style adds poll pressure to the action of the basic cross-under.

There are some bridles that have reins attached to a strap or rope that goes over the horse's nose. These add some pressure over the nose to the sidepull action.

When you are considering any cross-under or cross-over bridle it's worth taking into account the fact that horses' reactions to anything that closes on their head can vary. Most horses seem to do fine with these bridles, and they are widely used successfully, just be aware that all horses are different. Also look carefully at how the straps run through the rings when you take up the rein, and check that they release instantly as soon as you release. Apart from considering the comfort of your horse, it would be hard to have clear signals if the cross under action was sticky.

Pros:

- Some designs are liked because they look very similar to bitted bridles.
- Those designs that have an instant release give clear signals.

Cons:

- Many don't release instantly.
- Because of the closing action, they are not suitable for groundwork.
- Some horses do not like the poll pressure.
- Tightens on your horse's face.

Hackamore (Jaquima)

A hackamore, or jaquima, is used in the California Vaquero tradition. It may also be known as a western hackamore. There are two parts to it. The first part is the bosal, which sits on the horse's nose and is held in place by a simple leather hanger that goes over the ears. The second part is the mecate, which is a long "rope" that is traditionally made from horse hair. It is knotted to form the reins with a length spare at the side to make a lead rope. The mecate is freshly tied to the bosal each time you ride and removed when you finish.

You may also have heard of another type of hackamore, the mechanical hackamore. The mechanical hackamore would be more common in the UK. This is an entirely different device which we will discuss shortly.

I have ridden my horses for many years in a rope halter, but a few years back the time had come for me to transition to riding my horse Ozzie in a bosal and mecate (hackamore). As these are quite a sophisticated tool, first I needed to get one made that was of a high quality and fit my horse exactly.

Where to buy a hackamore

The hackamore is quite a historic tool with a lot of tradition behind it. It has to be made to a very specific method, with very specific materials being used.

A good hackamore is not cheap. This reflects the amazing quality of the materials and the years of experience and skill of the maker. Also the mecate is quite an investment as well. I like to use a horsehair mecate, but some people find them too prickly, although they do smooth and soften with use. There are alternatives, which can also be really good quality and some, such as alpaca, will cost more than horsehair.

It's a major investment but, cared for properly, your hackamore will last a lifetime. So it makes sense to buy from a reputable seller. Find someone who is recommended by the people who understand this tradition. They should ask for measurements of your horse's head and recommend the right fit for them.

It can be quite difficult to find a reputable bosal and mecate maker. Unless you go to a professional hackamore maker, most hackamores you see online, on ebay, on facebook, at shows, are not made correctly with the correct traditional material or with the correct traditional design. These will be useless to you, and a waste of your money. It is very common to find such examples at large horse shows and from general tack stores. I recently went to one of the largest horse shows in the world, and while there were a number of shops selling hackamores, none of them were suitable to use on a horse as they were all made with inferior materials or designed incorrectly.

Hackamore size

Normally a horse's first bosal would be a 5/8" bosal and as their education progresses their bosal can get thinner. When you attach the mecate to ride it becomes a hackamore. When used in combination with a bridle, as a "two rein" then it is simply referred to as a bosal.

Don't confuse the size of your horse's head or their breed with the size of hackamore you need. The diameter of the hackamore relates to their education level, and all horses should start off in a ⅝ inch hackamore.

- A larger diameter hackamore can be used to start a horse only if you have a ton of hackamore experience.
- A smaller diameter hackamore should be used for an advanced riding horse only if you, the rider, can ride all lateral movements perfectly, one handed, in all gaits with balance, lightness.

Don't think that you have to move to a smaller hackamore as you and your horse get more experience. Many of us will carry on in the ⅝ hackamore, there's not too much you can't do in one!

Hackamore construction

A bosal should always have a rawhide core, it should be flexible and it should feel smooth so that it won't rub the horse's fur.

The leather used must be the right type - rawhide is the most common - and there must be a high density of plaiting so that the bosal doesn't rub your horse's nose.

The fit must be precise and quite snug, which can't be achieved with a hard, unyielding bosal.

The bosal must be the right thickness for the level of education of your horse - too thick and it will be uncomfortable and heavy, too thin and it will be too harsh. When you hold both ends of the hackamore in your hand and squeeze you should be able to create a little wave in the noseband part, this tells you that you will be able to properly shape it.

Beware cheap bridle-hackamore hybrids with nosebands that look similar to a bosal but aren't the same quality. Some are made of nylon rope, or leather with a metal core. They are becoming quite fashionable in some circles. They won't work correctly in the way that a traditional hackamore is designed to and should be avoided.

A hackamore purchase has to be researched, recommendations of traditional makers obtained, and then ideally it will be custom made to fit your horse. A good hackamore maker will fall over backwards to help you make the right choice.

The mecate

The mecate rein is traditionally made of horsehair, but can be made of a variety of other materials including paracord, alpaca fibres and soft rope. They come in many different colours. The average length of a mecate is 22ft but they can be up to 30ft long.

The mecate (rein) should be the same diameter as the bosal. The bosal should be the right length to fit your horse with no more than 3 wraps of the mecate. It's quite science!

Hackamore fit

You'll need to shape your hackamore so it fits on your horse's nose snugly, like a hat fits on your head. I ride both my horses in a hackamore and I have two bosals and mecates. I have one hackamore for each horse as, while the same size hackamore would fit both, their faces are shaped differently. I need two hackamores with each one being shaped for each individual horse.

The bosal should fit as snugly to your horse's face as you can manage. It should sit above the end of the nasal bone and come to rest under the chin. When the mecate is correctly wrapped you shouldn't be able to get more than two fingers in the gap between the bosal and the horse's head. Take time to shape it correctly for your horse. This may involve mysterious binding with string and maybe careful positioning of a can of beans...

Why such precision? Because a properly adjusted bosal affects the entire face. This is completely different to the action of a snaffle bit for example and it means that we have to ride differently when we use one. If you pick up on your right rein the bosal will push on the left side of the face, for example. It also gives you very precise ask and release if used correctly.

Used well, the bosal works in a refined way on the horse's nose, meaning that you can use light vibration through your fingers to soften the poll or otherwise influence your horse. If your bosal is too big you lose the refinement. If a properly fitted bosal rubs your horse's head you are doing something wrong. You can't be riding with constant weight in your hands in a bosal, it's a tool that requires precise pressure and a real release.

Some will argue that a hackamore is "one size fits all" because it can be made to fit almost all horses by varying the number of wraps on the bosal and that you can never have too many wraps, I politely disagree. Others like the bosal to be rigid, heavier and some like it to bounce under the horse's chin when loping. I politely disagree with that as well. If you can see masses of daylight around a bosal then it will move about enough to cause discomfort to your horse.

A little while ago I was attending a clinic in the UK. A more advanced group of riders had assembled in the field for a lesson on riding in the hackamore. They were all warming up while the trainer watched. A rider rode over to him and drew his attention to the fact that even though she was very careful with her hands, her horse seemed unhappy and was tending to shake his head as she rode.

The trainer agreed that he had observed this and had been planning to speak to her. The hackamore was too long for her horse's nose and was moving about too much. It bounced whenever she went faster than a walk.

The rider admitted that she had suspected this was the problem. She was very frustrated because the hackamore had been 'fitted' for her horse by a person who sold them and had visited her yard. It hadn't been cheap either! They took it off and examined it. Not only was it too big, it was heavy and inflexible so it couldn't ever be shaped to a horse's head.

Luckily one of the other riders had a spare bosal in her lorry that she was happy to lend. It was a beautiful rawhide bosal from a reputable maker and it fitted the horse perfectly with just two wraps in the mecate. From then on horse and rider were able to enjoy the rest of the clinic and we were able to see how well they got on together when the horse was comfortable.

As the clinic drew to a close the rider was embarking on an interesting email correspondence with the person who had sold her the badly fitting bosal...

Hackamore care

Treasure your bosal! It should never be hung in your tack room by the hanger because the shape will become distorted. Remove the mecate after every ride to prevent that happening and coil it up to avoid it getting twisted. Keep it away from rodents and dogs because rawhide is very tasty to them!

Hackamore (bosal and mecate) pros and cons

Pros:

- Instant release.
- Doesn't tighten on your horse's face.
- Great for consistent and subtle cues when riding.
- Used also in groundwork.
- Voted the #1 type of bitless bridle to use for advanced riding goals by the Listening to the Horse community.

Cons:

- Riders need to be prepared to learn the correct riding style and often improve their riding skills and cues.
- Expensive to get a properly made one, as they are handmade.
- Cheap ones are useless and will cause discomfort to the horse. Do not buy one.
- Not suitable for riding with a constant contact.

Mechanical hackamore

It's worth mentioning briefly the other style of hackamore, which could be termed to be the mechanical hackamore. These hackamores involve some sort of metal attachment to the bridle and reins.

There are some simple mechanical hackamore options that are popular with bitless riders. An example of these would be the Flower Hackamore. This is circle with holes that allows the rider to adjust the position of the rein to exert more or less pressure on the nose and poll. Some Flower Hackamores have a short shank formed by two curved pieces of metal attached to the metal circle, which would allow you to have an option with stronger poll pressure.

You would need to make the decision on how much poll pressure you are comfortable using on your horse. Many are not happy to use poll pressure at all. If you have taught your horse to lower his head, maybe to put on the bridle, by touching his poll area, then this style of bitless bridle could confuse him.

Styles such as the English and German hackamores which involve longer shanks are quite a strong tool and are often used by riders who feel that they don't have enough control in a bit. I don't propose to discuss them here.

Bitless bridle fit issues

Finding the correct bitless bridle is not always an easy option. Here are some common fit and design issues that have been encountered by our students.

1. I tried a bitless bridle but its design made my horse claustrophobic. It applied so much pressure under the jaw and chin from it's criss/cross rein design that squeezed the horse's face. I would never recommend this design.
2. I started out with the cross under styles, which seemed to work fine at first, but my horses did not seem to like all the strapping on their heads and also the poll pressure those can generate. The rule seems to be less is more for me.
3. I've ridden with a mechanical hackamore that my horse seemed to prefer over a bit, but it was still too easy to put too much pressure (due to my inexperience) which resulted in her rearing once. No injuries, but it taught me a good lesson.
4. I have tried various rope halters. Off the shelf ones don't tend to fit very well. I think it is best to custom make your own, or you can end up with it sliding around a lot.
5. I sometimes ride in a rope halter but it's just not accurate enough for training.
6. Yes I've tried different rope side pulls and didn't like the nose band as they moved too far across the face, the chin straps were too long
7. I do not like a "bitless" that uses a long shank, ie english hackamore...put one across your shin and secure it... give it a pull and see how you like it.. you won't.

8. When I first transitioned to bitless I just bought a super cheap one for about £30. It was inflexible and I don't feel that it put pressure in the correct places.
9. Any California hackamore with a cable core is garbage.
10. I am not too fond of any mechanical hackamores. I have only tried a flower hack once; it felt too severe to me. Also you need to attach it to your horse's head pretty tightly so that it won't slip when riding. So in my opinion even at rest the horse doesn't have as much room as it does for example with a sidepull or rope halter.
11. Some of the bitless bridles don't give a good release. So even when you release the reins, there is no release of pressure on the face.

Homework:

Choose 2 styles of bitless bridles you would be interested in learning more about, and share your reasons why with a friend.

Contact and the bitless bridle

The bitless bridles I've mentioned are designed to work on pressure and release, so will be most effective if not ridden using a constant contact.

So if you are used to riding with a looser rein, or just a millimeter away from contact, then you will be starting in a great place.

If you are used to riding your horse with a constant contact, sometimes called an "English contact" this could be an opportunity to consider whether a constant contact is a strategy that is important for you to continue with in the future.

A bitless bridle can work with a constant contact, but, just as when riding with a bit, over time that will desensitise your horse to light aids.

Is groundwork preparation important?

The short answer is yes. It's not just about bitless bridles! It's about our partnership with our horse, and how well educated our horses are to ride. Putting a new device on your horse's head is not going to be a magic cue if your horse is leaning, heavy on the forehand or doesn't understand how to soften and bend. So it's as much about educating your horse, and oftentimes the rider as well, as it is using a different bridle.

- 94.3% of those surveyed in our community said riding bitless would be easier and more successful, if your horse had great groundwork skills (stop, turns, go, backup in a rope halter) BEFORE you did the switch to bitless.
- 87.7% of those surveyed in our community said riding bitless is likely to be easier if you had walked your horse in new places on foot, to develop communication and build their confidence in new places. So they will be less likely to get nervous, spook or bolt and you will be more confident and relaxed riding.

Whatever you have done with your horse before, you should check them out ridden without a bit, in a safe area to make sure that both of you will be safe. A surprising number of horses, even those who are strong in a bit, take to bitless riding really easily, but let's not make any assumptions. Doing suitable groundwork exercises is a very important factor in how successful your transitions to riding bitless will be.

Homework: Plan out 3 different groundwork exercises you want to improve with your horse. These will help you no matter if you ride with a bit or ride bitless.

The Saddle

The best saddle for you and your horse is the one that fits you both perfectly, but finding that saddle is often easier said than done. In my personal experience in Ireland with approximately fifteen saddle fitters in Ireland a few years back, I found only one saddle fitter in Cork who could accurately fit a saddle, to my satisfaction.

It started on a sunny day, as I was riding Ozzie in the paddock. He refused to walk forwards. I asked him again, and once again, a complete refusal to walk forwards!

As we were standing still together, in the middle of the paddock in Ireland, I remember thinking - this is really weird!

So I decided to dismount & see if I could figure out what was going on. However things were about to get weirder still!

As I usually do, to prepare to dismount from my baroque saddle, I took both of my feet out of the stirrups. Ozzie's head went up a little, but he stayed standing still. Then I put my reins in one hand, and moved my weight to prepare to dismount.

Ozzie immediately started to tense up & started walking backwards. I sat up tall again, and rubbed his neck, trying my best to figure out what was going on. Ozzie stood still again, and we both had a rest.

After a minute I once again tried to dismount, but Oz got even more worried, and again started to walk backwards, and got quite agitated.

At this point I knew there had to be some type of pain issue, and this behavior was completely out of character. But now Oz was worried & tense, and I was unable to dismount!

My only hope was to try & get him to relax. So I stayed there for about 5 minutes, and started singing to Ozzie while I sat in the saddle. I asked nothing of him. I just rubbed his neck, relaxed in the saddle, and sang my heart out.

As the minutes ticked by, I could feel his body start to relax.

After about five minutes, I stayed relaxed, but took my opportunity & did my best balanced dismount on the off side.

Long story short, it turned out the saddle didn't fit my horse. It was too narrow and was pinching his shoulders.

And subsequently after that, I ended up on the recommendation of two saddle fitters I had booked to come out & visit & fit my horse, purchasing two more saddles that didn't fit my horse. It was at that stage that I lost most of my faith in saddle fitters.

The bad news is that many of my horse friends in Europe, UK, Australia, Canada, the USA and beyond have had the same issues. It seems to be a worldwide problem.

It's really difficult to be able to find a saddle fitter you can trust, a saddle fitter who truly has the knowledge to fit a saddle correctly, and a saddle fitter who is happy to leave a yard without selling a saddle if the 20-30 saddles he has in his van do not fit the horse.

I've seen saddles which were said to 'fit' the horse by various saddle fitters – my own horse included – and which actually didn't fit the horse and caused pain.

Does my saddle fit?

The first step for any rider is to check if your saddle fits. Fingers crossed yours will be ok! Before and after you ride I recommend that you check your horses back for back pain. This can be a useful way to investigate for yourself whether there could be a potential saddle issue. This should become a routine for you. Here is the process I follow:

Your horse will be relaxed, and standing on a loose rope. Your horse will have the ability to move a few steps if they wish to. Your horse is not tied to cross ties or anything where their movement is restrained.

Run your hand over gently where the saddle would lie. Your horse should be able to be able to move away from you if they want to.

Look for any of these signs:

- Skin to twitch under your hand
- Horse to move a step
- Horse to turn his head around
- Try to bite
- Put his ears back
- Any type of reaction
- If you get a reaction, try again in that place and see if it was just a random reaction or if it happens again and you actually have an issue.

Quite often horses may have sore backs, but they are stoic and not letting us know that! So we need to check and look for subtle signs.

There are a lot of saddle fit issues out there in the world, and it's quite common for these to be an issue that the rider is not yet aware of. If there is any type of issue, you want to know immediately. I do this each time I ride my horses, Ozzie and Matilda.

Back health exercise

Check your horses back before and after each ride. Another important routine is to get an equine physiotherapist out to your horse, at least once a year or more often if you have a concern something might not be 100%, or if your horse's behaviour has changed. A physiotherapist or body worker will be able to tell you exactly where there is any type or pain, soreness or stiffness in your horse's body. This is very valuable information to have.

Homework: Schedule a physio or bodyworker visit at least once a year

The saddle must fit the horse

Imagine that you need to unlock the front door of your house. However someone took your front door key off its keychain, and instead put it into an old box of keys you had. This box holds over 100 different - all quite similar - house and door keys that you've used for various purposes over the last few years. Each of those 100 keys looks roughly the same, but each key is also unique, and has small differences from the other door keys.

If you try all those 100 keys in your front door, 99 of those keys will not work.

Only 1 key will fit the lock exactly.

It's the same with horse saddles. Regardless if you want an English, Western, Aussie stock saddle, endurance saddle, GP saddle or any other type of saddle.

I had a friend looking to buy a new western saddle for her horse. She went into a large tack shop and looked at more than 35 western saddles that she was given to understand would be the right fit for her height and size. Now full disclosure, their saddles were gorgeous! They were beautiful colours and felt really soft when she sat in them. However she knew that none of those 35 saddles would have fitted her horse. She walked out empty handed.

When you think about that a bit more, the chances of a saddle fitter visiting your house with five saddles in his car, and proclaiming that one of these five saddles fits both you and your horse perfectly, is unlikely.

Homework:

Rate the chances of one of 3 saddles from a tack shop fitting your horse and you correctly. 50%, 10%, highly unlikely indeed.

Unwanted behaviour that can be caused by the saddle

These symptoms could be caused by a bad saddle fit that is causing your horse pain:

- Not as good as he used to be when standing at a mounting block, moves around.
- Resting or lifting a front leg a little while standing still.
- Looks worried, tension in body, head goes up, when you prepare to dismount (painful around withers, saddle too narrow).
- Shoulders are very tight.
- Circles and bends are not good (pain or a jumping type saddle can restrict shoulder movement).

- Lateral training is not progressing / good (same reason as before).
- Bucking (could be saddle too wide and pressing down on horse's back).
- Standing still on a loose rein at halt, but when you rub your hand over his back he starts to walk off. See if you can identify which area of this back causes this to help figure out what part of the saddle is the issue.
- Behavior that is not normal for your horse.
- Any movement or pain expressed in his body or face when you rub his back. This may include ears back, trying to bite etc.
- Doesn't want to go forward.
- Doesn't want to trot.
- Lacking impulsion (to avoid impending pain from the saddle).
- Saddle moving around a lot on the horse.
- Reluctance to hack out.
- Difficulty taking a lead change.
- Horse has kicked your saddler.
- Difficulty putting a saddle on your horse.
- Rearing.
- Issues doing up the girth… horse not happy, foot stamping, biting, etc.
- Horse cannot move straight.
- Rider doesn't feel comfortable in the saddle.
- Rider looks like they are sitting in an armchair while in the saddle.

A lot of horses with pain from a saddle fit can continue on doing their jobs as normal as they will not tell you. To find out, get an equine physio, vet etc to check your horse next time you can find one – at your yard, a local event, etc.

A saddle fitter may have told you your saddle fits in the past. Do not assume this is correct information today. Your horse is constantly changing shape due to the time of year and the exercise they do. Any issues above could mean your saddle does not fit.

Homework:

Write down any unwanted behaviour you have noticed in any horse over the last 12 months, that could be a warning sign for a saddle fit issue.

3 mistakes to avoid when buying a new saddle

When my favourite saddle fitter came out to visit me and Ozzie he spent two hours explaining all of the different features that needed to be correct in order for any saddle to fit Ozzie. There were at least 20 things that needed to be designed in a specific way on any saddle for it to fit my horse correctly.

If I went through every point this would turn into a book on saddle fitting rather than horsemanship! However, I want to share with you three exercises you can do today to help improve the chances of finding a saddle that could fit your horse correctly.

Saddle width

One of the major things which needs to be correct, is to make sure the width of your saddle matches the width of your horse.

- If your saddle is too narrow, the saddle will be too high on your horse's back, and will pinch and hurt your horse's shoulders. You can get all types of unwanted behaviour when your horse is sore due to a narrow fitting saddle.
- If your saddle is too wide, and the underneath of the saddle where the gullet should allow extra room on the horse's back just about touches your horse, then it will not do its job of protecting your horse's vertebrae. Situations like this can cause you to get bucked off, or other unwanted behaviors.

So it's a very good idea, before any saddle fitter arrives, to have an idea if your horse is narrow, medium or wide. Different breeds can have certain anatomy characteristics, so that can help you work it out.

If you have a saddle that is too wide or narrow for your horse, unless it is an adjustable width saddle, you can't fix it. So you really want to avoid buying it in the first place!

The horse width exercise

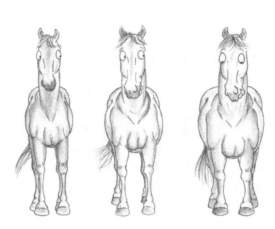

Look at least 3-5 horses. Look at your horses, friends' horses or any horses that are around. Stand carefully in front of the horse and look at their belly. Would you describe the general shape of the horse as narrow, medium or wide? Then move onto the next horse. The goal is to get your eye tuned into different horse shapes, so you can better judge your own horse.

My horse Ozzie, is a 14.3 Connemara and is definitely a wide type of horse. My horse Matilda, a 15.2 irish sports horse is also definitely a wide type of horse. So if someone told me I needed a narrow saddle, I would thank them and ask them to leave. The height of the horse doesn't directly correspond to saddle width either. You can have a narrow small pony and a very wide large warmblood type horse. Or you could have a wide shetland type pony, and a narrow thoroughbred horse.

The saddle width exercise

I want you to find as many saddles as you can. All sizes and types will do! It doesn't matter if they are English or western. If you can, put them sitting on any small barrels or saddle stands you have near you.

Then I want you to look at them all. Which ones look wider? Which ones look more narrow? Can you arrange the saddles from the most narrow to the most wide?

The saddle test exercise

While the rider is riding their horse at a walk in a safe environment, a second person should walk beside the horse's shoulder. They should be able to slide their hand in between the horse and saddle, below the withers where the saddle starts going down the horse's shoulder. As the horse walks on, the second person's hand will be squashed between the saddle and the horse's shoulder (which is fine). However as the horse walks forward, this person should feel no obvious 'pinch' sensation at the same point of each stride the horse takes.

So the width of the saddle needs to be checked first without a rider, and secondly with a rider.

Saddle length

The next step is to get a saddle that will be the correct length for your horse.

Each horse's back is a different length. Usually a small pony will have a shorter back than a large horse, which is understandable. If you have two similar horses - perhaps they are the same height and the same breed - they can also have two different length backs!

We need to make sure that the saddle you will use is not too long for your horse's back. Any style of saddle can be too long. There is quite a fashion for long western saddles, particularly those with square skirts.

There should be no weight on your horses back after the last rib. The last rib is attached to the 18th vertebrae of your horse. Any weight after this can't be supported and is very likely going to hurt your horse. If part of the rider's weight is put on the horse's back after the last rib it will cause soreness and possibly long-term damage for the horse.

The last rib exercise

Without any saddle on your horse, find the last rib on your horse's body. Here are three ways to do this.

- You can ask a bodyworker or your vet for help to find the last rib.
- You can do this by feeling for the horse's ribs along his side, and looking for the last one.
- On your horse's side, behind where your foot would be in a stirrup, look for the place where the horse's hair changes directions on his belly. Make a straight line from here straight up to the vertebrae along the top of your horse's back.

Mark the position of the last rib on your horse' body with chalk. Then put your saddle on your horse, without a numnah or saddle pad.

Does the back of the saddle touch the chalk? Would any part of the rider's weight be carried on or after that line of chalk?

If the answer is yes to both questions then your saddle is too long for your horse. This is a very common issue with many saddles. If you have a saddle that is too long for your horse, you can't fix it. So you really want to avoid buying it in the first place!

Saddle seat

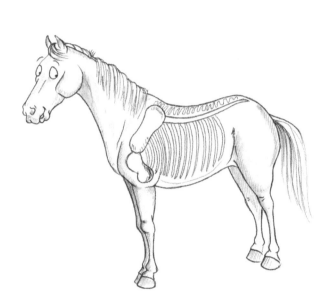

The horse's thoracic spine has 18 vertebrae. Each of those vertebrae has 2 ribs attached at the sides. All together these form the rib cage of our horse. The first vertebra is in front of where your saddle sits. The 18th vertebrae should be behind the weight bearing surface of your saddle.

The question is, where should you sit on the horse's back? To be in balance on the horse we need to be sitting on the strongest part of their back. This will minimise the potential to cause damage to their backs. It will also make them more free to perform athletically and in a way that is biomechanically correct.

The saddle seat exercise

Find the lowest part of your horse's back.

Ask your horse to stand still without a saddle. Draw a line with chalk on his back, where the lowest point of his back is. It is usually a little behind the withers. Take a photo of this.

Now put your saddle, without a numnah or saddle pad, on your horse back. Rock the saddle backwards and forwards a little, so that it settles into the most comfortable place on your horse's back. Take a photo of the saddle.

Compare both photos. The lowest point of your horse's back, which you marked with chalk, should be exactly the same as the lowest point of the saddle when it was on your horse's back.

The goal is for your saddle to naturally put the rider's weight in the same location as the lowest point of your horse's back. This is great for the horse as it is the strongest part of their back. This is great for the rider as it will dramatically improve your posture and help you to feel naturally more balanced when you ride. We want to avoid you sitting too far back on your horse's back, and encourage you to sit in a good position, avoiding falling into an 'armchair seat' with your legs out in front of your body.

Test drive your saddle

If you are confident that you have found a saddle that will fit your horse, the next step is to ask for a seven day trial. It is easy to get excited or slightly carried away when trying out a new saddle. Who doesn't love saddle shopping, right? If you try the saddle for 7 days, and take time to get used to it and monitor your horse's behaviour, and check their back before and after each ride, you will be increasing your chances that the new saddle might fit correctly.

One final note. Some people get made to measure saddles. Despite the promise, there is no guarantee that a made to measure saddle will fit when it is made, we still need to have the knowledge to check this ourselves.

Don't forget the rider

Now that we've discussed how the saddle should fit the horse, there is one more thing to think about before we move on. The saddle needs to fit the rider, and if the horse's back is going to remain healthy, the rider needs to fit the horse. It's a sensitive subject I know, but we are all responsible for ensuring that we are not too heavy to ride the horse we have. We need to look objectively at our own weight, add the weight of the saddle, and make sure that is within safe parameters for our horse. Once we have a saddle that fits our horse then we need to sit in it and get an objective view of whether we are properly positioned in it. This might be by asking the saddle fitter or a friend on the ground, or having someone take a photo to look at. All of the careful measuring and fitting will be for nothing if the rider's posterior is too big for the saddle seat, resulting in their weight coming down on the cantle. I don't propose to go into detailed discussion about correct rider to horse weight ratios, there is a lot of advice on this on the internet so you can look and come to your own conclusions.

The Rider

How we feel emotionally, and how we use our body has a dramatic impact on our horses when we are riding. Let's look at seven strategies that can help riders of all levels and disciplines.

- Improving your confidence level
- Using your reins less
- Using your weight and seat more
- Releasing tension in your body
- Looking where you want to go
- Being more aware of your breathing
- Improving your posture

Confidence levels

Earlier we explored how you can help your horse to build confidence using the comfort zones model.

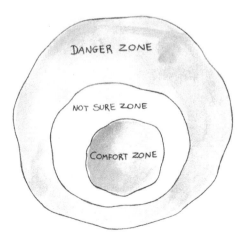

The 'comfort zone' is where your horse feels relaxed and happy. Comfort zones are often based around geographical areas - around the stables, their barn, and paddocks - places where their friends are.

When your horse is in a 'not sure' zone, your horse will not feel that confident or relaxed. Instead they can feel anxious or nervous. Their breathing may have got faster. They are starting to ignore you a little and are instead focused on or listening to something that is troubling them. They haven't panicked yet - but there's definitely a lot more anxiety going on. Often because the horse's level of worry and tension has increased, the human's will too.

The 'danger zone' is then when the horse thinks they're going to die. It is a life or death situation. In this zone, horses can react by running you over, bolting, spooking or other sudden movements. They are displaying an extreme lack of both confidence and relaxation. It is incredibly difficult to teach a horse anything useful when they are in the danger zone. It can also be very unsafe for the human so ideally we want to avoid putting our horses in the danger zone.

Now I want to apply this comfort zone model to you!

The comfort zone exercise

I would like you to get your colouring pencils out, as we are going to create some artwork. We are going to draw a map of your comfort zones when you are riding your horse.

Here are the 4 simple steps that I use:

- Get a piece of white paper, and a pen or pencil.
- Draw a basic map of where you can ride your horse. Include all paddocks, laneways, roads, trails, arenas etc that are on or around the property. Also include other places, like travelling to a friend, going to a horse show, clinic or event, or anywhere you would like to ride your horse away from home in the future.
- Get three coloured pencils or markers.
- Identify all the areas you feel comfortable to ride in, and color them green.
- Identify all the areas you are not so comfortable riding in, and color them orange.
- Identify all the areas you do not feel comfortable riding in, and colour them in red.

The idea is to ride mainly in the green areas, to not ride very often in the orange areas, and to avoid riding in the red areas, where you have no confidence.

This comfort zone map works hand in hand with your horse's comfort zone map you created in previous homework. It's likely that the comfort zones when riding will be very similar to how they looked for your horse when you are on the ground. However you might notice that your horse's comfort zone on the ground was bigger than it is when ridden.

So now you will use your map to plan where you are going to ride your horse.

How will your confidence increase?

- When you work to build your horse's confidence using their comfort zone map your confidence will naturally increase as you see and feel your horse getting more relaxed.
- When you limit your riding mostly to your comfort zone you will take a huge pressure off your shoulders. This will help you to relax more.
- As you ride successfully in your comfort zone your confidence will naturally start to increase also. Your original comfort zone area will slowly start to expand.

When you are using the comfort zone model it's interesting to notice your confidence levels growing in different locations. Very often you will see some substantial increases in your confidence levels. I would recommend that you redraw the map every 6-8 weeks, or even sooner, and see how far you have come.

Homework: Comfort zone check in

Redraw your comfort zone map in 6-8 weeks.

Using less rein cues

I was riding my horse Matilda one day and we were working on leg yields. However, they weren't really going very well. There seemed to be some sort of miscommunication between Matilda and I about what I was asking her to do. I decided to take a break for a few minutes. She did a big sigh, and we stood quietly in the middle of the arena, having a rest. My brain was whirling around, trying to figure out what the issue could be.

I thought about Matilda. I know that she is a horse who really wants to learn. I know she is very focused and tries really hard for me. So obviously she wasn't the issue here. The problem had to be something I was doing, or not doing.

I started to consider how I could ask her to do a leg yield in an easier way. I had two options:

- I could either make the cues bigger - which is not really what I ever wanted to do.
- Or I could make the cues easier to understand. So that meant really not using my legs very much, UNLESS I wanted them to be a specific cue!

When I was ready, I asked Matilda to walk around the arena again.

This time I was very aware of what my legs were doing. I made a big effort to not use them randomly. Quite often as riders our body is automatically doing things when we ride, but we have zero awareness that our hands or legs just did a certain movement.

So I did a few circles in a walk with Matilda. I was very conscious to use no leg cues. My goal was to keep my legs lying quietly by her side, and to release all tension in my legs. After a few minutes I asked her to leg yield again by looking where I wanted her to go, which naturally changed my posture and balance, and I touched her the tiniest bit with one leg.

She did it!

Matilda moved into a beautiful floaty leg yield across the paddock. I was speechless. She literally floated across the arena.

Matilda taught me a hugely important lesson that day. In general, it was to do less. This makes the difference between when you are not asking your horse to do anything and when you are asking in a way that is really clear for them. Your cues will be much clearer to your horse and it will be much easier for them to understand that you are asking for something.

A few days later I was riding Ozzie, my Connemara. With Ozzie I had a totally different situation, but the cause was again a problem with my legs!

Ozzie is quite an economical horse. He likes to take it easy. Anytime I ask Ozzie to transition from a walk to a trot there are a few things that will cause an issue and usually stop him from trotting.

One main one that hinders us is when I put any type of pressure on him with my two legs. When I squeeze with both of my legs, it causes Ozzie to slow down.

Think about it from Ozzie's perspective. When I squeeze both of my legs together I restrict the movement of his barrel. I make it harder for him to allow his barrel to swing from side to side. The barrel movement in Ozzie's body is directly connected to his hind feet.

When the barrel of the horse slows down the steps that the hind feet take slow down also. This means that the whole horse slows down.

A really useful goal to work towards is to start using your legs at the moments you need them for a cue, and not using them too much any other time. It will greatly improve your communication with your horse and it will allow your horse to move more freely.

The leg awareness exercise

Ride your horse in a few figures of eights and circles, as you normally would. I want you to notice what your legs are doing. How often do your legs move on one circle? Do you need to constantly move your legs to keep your horse going forwards? Do you think you could in any way have taught your horse to ignore your leg cues?

As you ride, focus on your legs and see if you can recognise any tension you carry in your legs. Think of your right leg - I want you to breathe out deeply and release all tension in that leg. Then do the same for your left leg.

Riding one handed

As riders we all have developed various habits around how we hold the reins, and how and when we use our reins. However, in order to improve our riding skills, we actually need to stop relying on our reins so much! Having a 'reins first' approach, is not going to help our balance or our horses' balance.

Instead we need to get much better at using our seat and leg and weight cues. When you ride like this it actually makes a lot more sense to the horse. So things can happen a lot easier.

One very effective way to help us break our bad habits is to adopt a new habit.

So experiment with a new habit of riding your horse one handed. To do this, both of your hands will be close together at the pommel, but only one hand will hold the reins. This hand will send small signals down the reins to your horse, when you move your fingers.

Your spare hand will be very close to your other hand. It can do nothing, or you can hold the part of the reins above your holding hand. The biggest mistake I see when someone does this is that the spare hand is doing random large movements. It should not. Your spare hand needs to be close to the pommel and the middle of your body, so your weight balance in the saddle stays level.

When I mention 'riding one handed' I want to clarify that I am not referring to 'neck reining'. Riding one handed and in balance can be seen in a few traditions around the world including the California Vaquero tradition, and when riding with a garrocha in Spain.

This style of one handed riding is not common, but it is a hugely powerful strategy to help all riders improve their cues and posture and to fix bad habits of over using their reins.

Kecia from the US enjoyed her one handed riding experience.

"One handed figures of eights - well now that was interesting doing them one handed! It felt a little uncomfortable but with that being said, I felt more balanced. I tend to sometimes have chicken wing arms and have been working to improve my posture. Riding one handed will definitely help me." Kecia, USA.

Riding one handed exercise

Ride a circle one handed with your horse. Both hands should be very close together, just in front of the saddle and very close to the withers. Hold the reins in one hand. Do not put your spare arm up in the air, or down at your side. Do not neck rein. Walk the circle like this and notice if this change in riding style requires you to use your seat and weight a lot more than normal.

Your seat

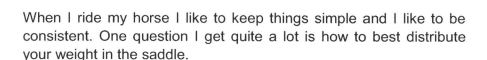

When I ride my horse I like to keep things simple and I like to be consistent. One question I get quite a lot is how to best distribute your weight in the saddle.

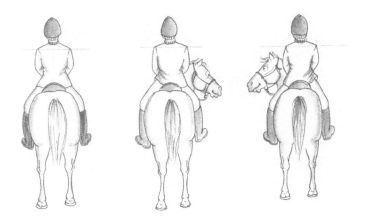

- When my horse is travelling on a straight line my weight is equally distributed on both of my seat bones.
- When my horse has a bend in his body (perhaps he is turning a corner, or on a circle) then I lift a little bit of weight off outside seat bone (the seat bone on the outside of the bend) By doing this there is a fraction more weight on my inside seatbone (the inside of the bend).
- For example, when I am doing an anti-clockwise circle, I lift a tiny bit of weight off my right seatbone.

- When I am doing a clockwise circle I lift a tiny bit of weight off my left seatbone.

If I would like my horse to create a bend in his body, all I need to do is lift one seatbone. This bend is useful for lots of moves including:

- Balanced turns and corners
- Leg yields
- Shoulder in and out
- Circles
- Figure of eights
- Hindquarters in and out
- Half pass
- Pirouettes.

The great benefit of doing it this way is that you can ask the horse to create a bend in their body without using your reins or your legs! I ride Matilda and Ozzie following this approach and it works beautifully. My horses change the bend in their body just from me adjusting my weight in the saddle.

The weight in saddle exercise

- Ride your horse in a straight line. Make sure you have equal weight on both seat bones. Ask a friend to watch you and confirm your seat is level, your shoulders are also level and you are looking straight ahead.
- Ride your horse in a circle going to the left. Lift a tiny bit of weight off your right seatbone.
- Ride your horse in a circle going to the right. Lift a tiny bit of weight off your left seatbone.

When you start doing this it will feel odd. However with practice it will become like muscle memory and it will become a habit that you are consistent with and do automatically.

Common mistake to avoid:

When your weight is slightly lifted off one seat bone don't collapse your ribs and don't tilt your shoulders.

Using our legs

While my weight in the saddle influences the bend in the horse's body, then my legs control the direction I ask my horse to move in.

- When my horse is travelling in a straight line my legs are in the same place - on both sides of the horse's body.
- When I would like to ask my horse to turn right I put my right leg back a fraction and my left leg forwards a fraction.

- When I would like to ask my horse to turn left I put my left leg back a fraction and my right leg forwards a fraction.

The great benefit of doing it this way is that I can ask my horse to change directions without using the reins. All I need to do is change the position of my legs. I ride Matilda and Ozzie following this approach and it works beautifully.

The changing direction exercise

Use your legs to change your horse's direction

- Ride your horse in a straight line. Make sure your legs are in the same place on both sides of the horse's body.
- Ride your horse in a circle going to the left. Put your left leg back a fraction, and your right leg forwards a fraction.
- Ride your horse in a circle going to the right. Put your right leg back a fraction and your left leg forwards a fraction.

When you start doing this it will feel odd. However with practice it will become like muscle memory and it will become a habit that you are consistent with and do automatically.

Posture

Making more use of our legs and weight in the saddle is a great way to improve our riding skills and both our balance and our horse's balance. However, when we do this we need to make sure our shoulders are not doing anything strange...

The still shoulders exercise

You are sitting in the saddle and your horse is standing still. Have a friend nearby watching you.

- Put your right leg back a fraction and your left leg forwards a fraction.
- Put your left leg back a fraction and your right leg forwards a fraction.
- Lift a tiny bit of weight off your right seatbone.
- Lift a tiny bit of weight off your left seatbone.

When you do all four of these movements the goal is that your friend cannot see any movement in your shoulders, or anywhere else in your body, except for your leg movement.

Freedom of movement

One day I was riding Ozzie in the fields when I noticed that there was something funny going on. While his walk was fine, there was no lameness or anything, he wasn't really striding out in the big ground covering walk that I know he is able to do.

When I am asking my horse to walk it's valuable to me to be able to ask my horse to do a slow walk, a medium speed walk and a big ground covering power walk!

So we stopped for a minute in the middle of the field. I started to wrack my brain to figure out what I could do while I was riding Ozzie, to help this to happen. Firstly, I assumed that I was probably blocking Ozzie's forward motion somehow. I must be doing something with my body. But the question was what exactly I was doing?

I know there are a few places I tend to carry tension in my body, so I decided to relax my lower back and really focus on allowing my lower back to move with the movement of the saddle. Wow! I got an immediate and huge response from Ozzie.

It was as if he was thinking *'Finally, Elaine, you took off the handbrake! I've been telling you to do that for the last ten minutes!'*

Ozzie's walk completely changed! Now he was doing a good impression of an 18 hands horse doing a forwards walk! We had power, relaxation, huge strides and a happy Connemara out on an adventure. It felt amazing.

The lower back exercise

Relax your lower back

Your homework is the next time you ride your horse - think about your lower back. I want you to breathe out and release any tension that you are holding there. Allow your hips to freely follow the movement of the saddle. For the second part of this work, I want you to observe what effect this has on your horse's movement.

Sight & focus

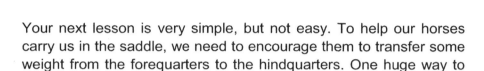

Your next lesson is very simple, but not easy. To help our horses carry us in the saddle, we need to encourage them to transfer some weight from the forequarters to the hindquarters. One huge way to mess this up is to look down when you ride your horse.

Our heads are very heavy. When we look down when we ride it also causes our whole bodies to lean forwards a little which dumps extra weight on the horse's shoulders and front legs. This is something we want to avoid at all costs.

I know looking down is a habit that is so common among horse riders. Here is your homework to fix this!

Look where you're going exercise

- Challenge 1: Ride one circle without looking down once.
- Challenge 2: Ride one figure of eight without looking down once.
- Challenge 3: Mount your horse and stand still. Then ride for five minutes, without looking down even once from the moment you mounted your horse. Your only goal for this session is never to look down. You can do any movements you wish, in any gaits you wish. The first time you try this challenge I recommend you do simple movements in walk.

Breathing

Have you ever been trotting or cantering your horse and when you stop you realise that you either have a red face or have ended up a bit out of breath? Or maybe you are getting a lesson, and you concentrate so hard on getting things right that you stop breathing?

It's really odd, but these are common issues for riders! It's disastrous for our horse riding! When we hold our breath the oxygen levels in our blood start to decrease. This means that our brain and organs do not receive the oxygen they need to function. The first symptoms are a feeling of confusion, altered decision making, and loss of coordination. All of which are not a good idea when you are trying to improve your riding!

"I had some issues with my horse bucking me off in our early days together. We figured out that it was an issue he was having with worms, and once that was fixed we never had another bucking issue. However, I was terrified to get on him. Not to ride him, just the act of getting on. I would put my foot in the stirrup, swing my leg over and wait for the explosion. It never came, but every time I stepped onto the mounting block I would be in full panic mode. I realized that I was taking a sharp intake of breath just as I would put my foot in the stirrup, then hold my breath as I got on. I reconditioned myself to very consciously and audibly breathe out just as I put my foot in the stirrup, which helped both my horse and me feel more relaxed. I will happily get off and back on now anywhere, without worrying, but I always breathe out just as I get on." Jocelyn.

The breathing exercise

- Ride your horse in 3 circles on a walk. I want you to breathe in slowly and then breathe out slowly and count your breaths. As you do this exercise your main focus will be your breathing.
- Ride your horse in a circle in walk, a circle in trot and then a circle in walk. Count how many seconds you breathe in and out in walk. Count how many seconds you breath in and out in trot. Does the rhythm of your breathing change when you get ready to trot? Or when you ask for a trot? Or when you are trotting? Can you complete this exercise from walk to trot to walk, with absolutely no change to your breathing pattern?

"I used to suffer from a classic freeze response when riding, particularly whilst hacking and usually for no obvious reason. I didn't think it was fair to allow my anxiety to make my horse feel anxious - I wanted him to feel relaxed and happy! I started using the simple breathing technique of breathing in for a count of 4 and out for seven. I found that whilst doing this, my horse would gently blow out through his nostrils and lower his head. It certainly worked for both of us and we happily hack out alone and in company now." Sue, UK

The Horse

The exercises I have learned over the last few decades have come from many different branches of equestrian sport. But the one thing that they have in common is that they are all beneficial for the horse.

I know many riders will be reading this book and will be from all over the USA, Europe and Australia, Canada and beyond. If you are a dressage rider, love trail rides or endurance, follow natural horsemanship or the Californian Vaquero traditions, ride English or Western - all of the riding exercises I am about to share will benefit both you and your horse hugely.

Much of the success you will see with your horse, will come primarily from 'how you do' rather than 'what you do'. With this in mind, before you try any of the following riding exercises with your horse, I'd advise you to quickly recap the cornerstones section in this book. Here are some philosophies to bear in mind:

- We want to do activities that will build the horse's trust.
- We want to break 1 big goal down into 100 mini-goals.
- We want to allow the horse to choose.
- We focus on helping the horse, not making the horse. This is especially important when in difficult situations.
- Allow the horse to rest often, and be generous with your words of praise.
- Go at the horse's speed. Quite often this is a lot slower than the speed we would choose ourselves.
- Be kind to the horse.
- Be kind to ourselves.

Homework:

Choose two philosophies you will focus on with your horse over the next 7 days.

The Holy Grail of Horse Riding

Let's go back to the basics. A horse has four legs. (I know, bear with me!)

Depending on if the horse is walking, trotting or canter, those legs are going to take different steps at different times.

- When a horse walks all four legs move at different times.
- When a horse trots, the front right (off) and the hind left (near) legs move at the same time. And the front left (near and the hind right (off) legs move at the same time.
- When a horse canters, one hind leg goes on its own, then a diagonal pair (two legs) move together), then the last fore leg moves.

Many riders know the sequence of legs in different gaits. But most riders also stop there - and never connect WHEN they ask their horse to do something - to the EXACT movement of those legs!

This timing of WHEN you ask your horse - in relationship to EXACTLY what foot is moving in what way - is the holy grail of horse riding.

And 99% of horse riders have never heard of it!

Crazy, right?

Happily you will soon be part of the 1% of horse riders who are in on the secret. So let's go!

Footfall sequence exercise

Draw the sequence of footfall in walk trot and canter

Footfall

Anytime you want your horse to go forwards, or turn, or step backwards, if you can ask them at the *split second* when that specific leg is about to leave the ground, it's very easy for the horse to follow your direction.

I want you to imagine this situation:

Your horse is walking along. He has just put ALL his weight on the right fore hoof. If you ask your horse to turn right as he is walking, just at that moment when ALL his weight is on his right (off) front foot, it will make no sense to him.

In fact, your bad timing can have negative consequences!

- It can easily unbalance your horse (and unbalanced horses turned into worried horses quite quickly).
- It makes it difficult for your horse to do what you are asking them.
- It also communicates to the horse that your timing is not very good.
- It could even feel to the horse like you're trying to trick them!

So today you are going to learn the first step in the process to improve your awareness of where your horses feet are.

Once you know where each foot is in motion - at any time - your timing is going to get a lot better. And you'll see your riding skills get a ton better and your cues in the saddle get much smaller and more subtle. Your horse will breathe a huge sigh of relief, that you've finally 'got it'!

I'd like you to imagine that your horse's rib cage area is shaped like a barrel. Maybe it's a beer barrel - you choose what is sort in it!

So when you sit on your horse, you're sitting on a barrel of your favourite beverage. So far so good! And as your horse walks around, that barrel swings a little from right to left.

Footfall exercise 1: Swing

As you ride your horse, focus on feeling the swing of the barrel as your legs naturally move side to side.

As you ride your horse in walk, I want you to feel the barrell swing right and left, over and over again, underneath the saddle. Feel your horse's rib cage move towards and away from each of your legs.

Footfall exercise 2: Standing

Your horse has two hind feet. As the horse walks around, each hind foot will take a step forward under the barrel. Here is the important thing - in order for this hind foot to reach forward and land under the barrel, the barrel of the horse has to move out of its way.

Footfall exercise 3: Visualisation

Close your eyes and imagine you are sitting in the saddle. When the horse's near hind steps forwards, deep under the horse's body, the barrell swings from left to right.

When the horse's off hind steps forwards, deep under the horse's body, the barrell swings from right to left.

So when your horse's hind feet are moving along in walk naturally, they are causing the barrel of the horse to swing gently right to left to right, and on and on.

- When the horse's near hind is under his body, the barrel has swung over to the right, to make room for that near hind foot.
- When the horse's off hind is under his body, the barrel has swung over to the left, to make room for that off hind foot.
- When your horse's hind legs are both the same (no one is further ahead of the other) the barrel of the horse will be directly under the saddle.

So at halt, just by noticing where the barrel of the horse is under your saddle, you can tell if the hind legs are standing square or are level with each other, because you will be able to feel the barrel being 100% centered under your saddle.

Footfall exercise 4: Stand still barrel exercise

The next time you are riding your horse, I want you to walk your horse, and then ask them to stand still on a loose rein. Feel if your horse has both hind feet level with each other, or if one hind foot is more forwards than the other.

The next foot strategy

We can also use this knowledge to tell us which is the next hind foot that your horse is going to use.

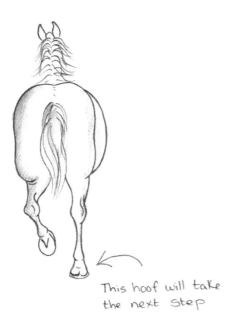

This hoof will take
the next step

Imagine the near hind leg is more forward, and the barrel of the horse will feel like it has swung to the right a little underneath your saddle. If you asked your horse to walk forwards at this moment, he will probably take the first step with his off hind leg - as that is the furthest back.

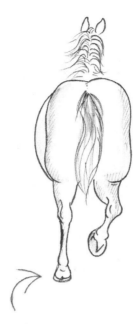

This hoof will take
the next step

Imagine the off hind leg is more forwards - because the barrel of the horse will feel like it has swung to the left a little, underneath your saddle. So if you asked him to walk forwards, he will probably take the first step with his near hind leg, as that is the furthest back at halt.

When I use this information as I am riding Ozzie and Matilda I can sit at a halt and tell which hind foot my horse will walk off with.

Footfall exercise 5: Which hind foot will step first?

- Ride your horse in walk and feel the barrell swing naturally left and right.
- Ask your horse to stop and then guess which hind leg they will use next were you to ask them to walk on again.

Once you figure this out (and it may take reading this a few times and then trying it out a few times to wrap your head around it) you are starting to connect the movement you can feel in the saddle through your legs to the location of your horse's hind feet.

You will be able to tell which hind foot is going to take the next step, without needing to look at the hind feet.

I promise you, when you figure this out, your horse will love you!

Improving direction

Sometimes the direction you would like your horse to go isn't quite the direction your horse is choosing! This is a fun exercise to help your horse to change how he thinks.

I like to do this exercise along a fence line or in an arena. You can also do this exercise anywhere you have an obvious track you can follow (either a path in the grass, or maybe you can set up a rectangle shaped area with some poles on the ground).

Imagine you are riding your horse on a loose rein, it could be in walk or trot around the perimeter or the arena. But your horse wants to leave the perimeter and go to the inside of the arena. Or they would prefer to leave the track and go somewhere else.

If you are riding them on a loose rein, it's easy to notice this.

If you are riding with a straight line between your hand and your horses mouth, or you are using your legs are lot to adjust your horse, please change your cues, use less leg and relax your hands, so you can get more feedback from your horse on what direction (if allowed) he would like to move towards.

When you have a loose rein, you give the horse the choice. Then you gain valuable information.

I was working on this one day with Ozzie my Connemara. As I was trotting around on a loose rein, I noticed that when we were going clockwise he was happy to stay moving in the direction I asked him. However when we were going anti-clockwise, he would want to leave the track a few times each lap and come into the centre of the arena.

If I just tried to only use pressure on the reins or from my legs to ask Ozzie to trot and stay on the perimeter going anti clockwise - we'd just end up arguing with each other. That's not what I want at all!

So I needed to change how Ozzie was thinking. If I could change how he was thinking, then his behaviour would automatically change.

When Ozzie decided he wanted to turn to the left and come into the arena, I tried a different strategy. I let him do it but immediately we did a small circle to the left (which is hard work for Ozzie) and then went back out to the perimeter of the original track again.

We kept doing this on a loose rein (with many small left circles each time Ozzie chose to turn away from the perimeter) until he did a full circle without deciding he needed to turn into the middle of the arena.

It took a couple of minutes on this occasion. If you had to work on something like this you could also break the process down and work over a few days if need be. Work with what your horse is ready to do and recognise small wins. If your horse comes away from the perimeter on average 5 times per lap, a great success for one day would be for him to just do this 4 times!

It's always about little steps. I find horses think a lot about things between sessions. Often they come back on day 2 much better than where we ended on day 1. Time to think is really important for a horse.

Ozzie and I repeated this exercise on a loose rein over a few days. Now, we can trot around the perimeter happily on a loose rein, in both directions, and Ozzie chooses to stay on the perimeter track.

And there are huge benefits to this:

- Your horse is not trying to take over.
- You are not being tempted to pull on the reins to correct your horse.
- You and your horse are now thinking the same thing.
- Don't have to keep doing lots of little corrections.
- Your horse's main focus isn't going in a random direction any more.
- There is more focus, more communication, more connection.

Here are some common mistakes to avoid:

- There should be no change in your emotions, no matter what your horse chooses to do.
- Don't get annoyed or angry.
- Don't lose patience.
- Make sure your body stays relaxed, don't tighten up.
- Don't do it a few times and give up! On day 1 all you're looking for is a tiny change. Maybe at the start they would leave the perimeter 6 times on every lap, but now they only do it 5 times. That's huge progress!
- Recognise and be thankful for tiny improvements, because that means you're on the right path.

Perimeter track exercise

Try out this perimeter exercise with your horse. First ride in a safe place, with a little slack in the rein, and see what direction your horse really wants to travel in. Take this information, work a bit in both directions, then proceed to doing a small circle each time your horse leaves the perimeter, until they return back to the perimeter again.

Fun with Cones

I love using cones when I ride my horses. Here is one of my favourite riding exercises to improve your transitions and accuracy. You will need two cones.

2 Cones exercise

Put two cones close together about a metre apart, in the middle of your paddock or arena.

You will ask your horse to trot a figure of 8. In the middle of the figure of 8 you will ride through the two cones.

The moment you ride through the two cones, you will go back to walk for three steps. Then you will move forwards into trot again.

This is a really fun exercise. And it's nice to do this with friends as well! This is a great way to have fun, improve your accuracy and transitions and have fun together.

Here are some tips that might be useful:

- When going back to walk, I would explore how much you can do with your seat and weight, breathe out loudly, sit on the back pockets of your jeans and also see how little you can do with your reins.

- Then when going from walk to trot, make sure you look where you want to go and bring the life up in your body. So it's more that the horse will start to follow your energy.
- Also count the steps your horse takes. Once you start to ask - how many steps does it take for your horse to go back to walk? After you do this a few times, does your horse need less steps? You can do the same when asking your horse to move from walk to trot also.

8 Cones exercise

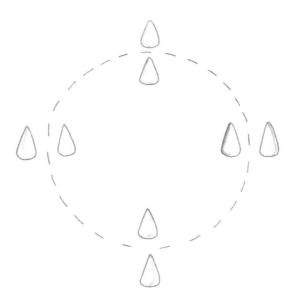

Set up a circle, using 8 cones as in the picture above. Each pair of cones can be around 1 meter apart. The aim is to ride a circle, going through each pair of cones.

You can begin this in walk, in both directions. Notice if one direction is easier for your horse than the other. Repeat this in trot and then afterwards, repeat this in canter.

This is a great exercise to help with your accuracy and get closer to not having egg shaped circles!

A useful tip would be to make the circle quite large to start off with, to make it easier for the horse. Large circles are much easier for horses, than small circles.

Fun with Polework

Have you ever tacked up your horse, sat in the saddle, and then paused and wondered what you should do today? Well, you're not alone!

It's very hard to have an unlimited stream of fun yet hugely beneficial groundwork and riding exercises up your sleeve!

I have a tip for you that has helped me a lot with Ozzie and Matilda. With just a few wooden poles - which you can pick up at a local hardware store, you can turn your riding from 'uneventful and repetitive' to 'fun and engaging'. And you can add a LOT of creativity into your time with your horse.

"We set out the triangle and spider and did them in hand yesterday, and ridden in walk today. Ruby can get anxious and speedy over poles so I worked on just walking over them in all different directions in a relaxed fashion with plenty of breaks and she did really well. Several other people came to see what we were doing and loved these polework exercises too!" Jane, UK.

It's no secret that I love pole work exercises! Here are some polework exercises you can have fun with.

Polework exercises

Complete these polework exercises at a walk or trot with your horse.

Narrow 1

POLEWORK EXERCISES
TRAINING

Arrow 1

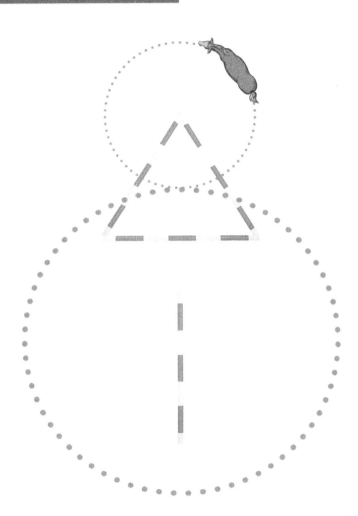

www.greyponyfilms.com

Pyramid 1

POLEWORK EXERCISES
TRAINING

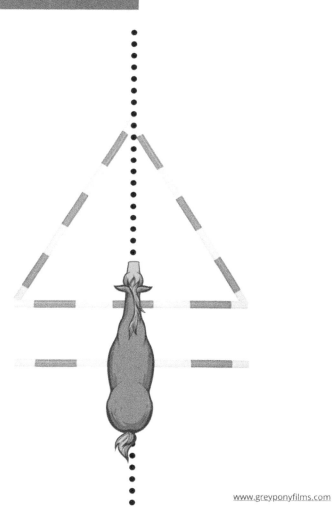

www.greyponyfilms.com

The H 1

POLEWORK   EXERCISES

TRAINING

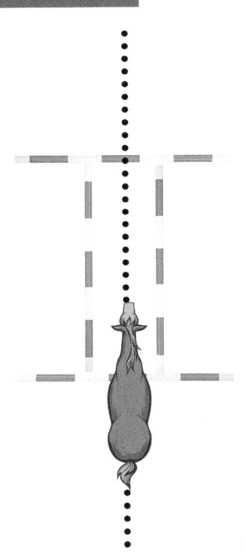

www.greyponyfilms.com

The fast horse

It was a beautiful day in Ireland. So I decided to tack up Ozzie and go for a ride in the fields. The weather was perfect - warm and sunny. In my head I had images of Ozzie and I doing effortless half passes across the field. It was going to be great!

As we started to walk up the field, I could feel that Ozzie was just as excited as I was. He had a ton of energy! Instead of walking, in fact he wanted to trot! However, he was also pushing forwards, ignoring my cues to ask him to relax and slow down, and the reins felt heavy in my hands. So I had to abandon my half pass plan and change to a new plan asap! Ozzie was offering me a lot more energy than I needed. I needed to help him to decide that going fast up the field wasn't the best decision for him to make.

I decided on a new strategy to help him work out that going forwards fast wasn't the best option right now. I allowed him to set the speed, but I took charge of the direction.

In the field where I was riding there were lots of daisies. So I asked Ozzie to walk in hundreds of tiny circles around all these little plants. Each circle was about 4 or 5 steps. When a circle was complete we changed direction and found another little daisy plant to circle around.

We spent about five minutes doing a lot of daisy circles, with a different direction for each circle.

Ozzie still had the choice to keep doing a very fast walk around these daisies and for a while that's what he did. Once he realised that all we were doing was staying in the same place, walking round daisy plants, his energy levels started to wane. He began to both relax and slow down a little.

When I could feel him relax and actually be open to standing still, I relaxed in the saddle and did a deep breath out. Ozzie stopped walking and stood still, without me touching the reins. That was something that would not have been possible five minutes previously when he wanted to go fast up the field.

He stood still for about 30 seconds, but I could feel his energy level go up again. Ozzie decided to start walking by himself, so back to plan B again. Around all the daisy plants we went for the second time, in heaps of tiny circles, changing direction after each little circle. This time it took about three minutes walking around the daisies for Ozzie to decide that he was OK to relax and slow down again. Once again, I relaxed in the saddle and did a deep breath out. Ozzie stopped walking and stood still, without me touching the reins.

This time we stood still together for about a minute and then he set off. Back to plan B again. Around all the daisy plants we went for the third time, in heaps of tiny circles, changing direction after each little circle.

We kept this up for about 20-25 minutes and by the end of the session Ozzie was so much more relaxed, focused and listening to me. It's really a magical feeling when your idea becomes your horse's idea.

I decided to quit on a good note and work on my half-passes some other day. There was no rush.

Daisy circles exercise

Find an opportunity when your horse is offering you more energy than you are asking for. Practise your daisy circles. Be aware of when your horse is slowing down naturally and is offering to stop. Allow the horse to stop and rest. When the horse decides he needs to move forwards again, repeat the daisy circles.

The energy efficient horse

Sometimes riders need to deal with the opposite issue. Their horse is quite relaxed and economical, and asking them to hurry up is a challenge!

Matilda and I did a fun exercise one day with a friend of mine, who was riding a lovely horse called Hamish. On that day both Matilda and Hamish were pretty relaxed, so there wasn't a lot of excess energy going around! We decided to do a walking race.

We put two cones up at the top of the arena. Both horses had to start together, do as fast a walk as possible up to the cones, turn around the cone and then do a fast walk back to where we started.

Nothing like a little healthy competition to encourage the riders to change their energy! And when the riders' energy changed, so did their horses.

The only rule was if your horse broke into a trot you had to go back to the start and begin the race again. It was a lot of fun, we had a few spectators cheering us on and I think both horses and riders had big smiles on their faces for the entire race.

The winner was Hamish! It was a great day.

Walking race exercise

Set up a walking race with a friend. Map out a short course. The only rule is that if any horse trots they have to go back to the beginning and start again. Have fun!

The Balance Bootcamp

One of the biggest things that will hold you back from progressing with your riding is having a horse who tends to carry a lot of weight on their front two legs, who pulls on the reins, or feels heavy on the reins when you are riding.

The problem here is a balance issue.

I have a simple exercise to help your horse to start to carry a little more weight on their hind two legs, improve their balance and to feel a little lighter in your hands.

Sounds good? Let's get started.

The 10-9-8 exercise

This riding exercise is called the 10-9-8 exercise.

The goal is that you can ask your horse to:

- Walk 10 steps forward
- Walk 10 steps backwards
- Walk 9 steps forwards
- Walk 9 steps backwards
- And so on until..
- Walk 1 step forwards
- Walk 1 step backwards
- Shift their weight forwards without moving a foot
- Shift their weight backwards without moving a foot.

Sounds simple, but it's not easy!

First, you will need to break this exercise down and just do a little bit at a time. When I began this with Ozzie I had to do one or two moves (eg. 4 steps forwards, 4 steps backwards) and then give him a rest and allow him to stand still on a loose rein for about 30 seconds. He would do the largest yawns you have ever seen!

It was really important to Ozzie that he got this time to process what we had just done. So one day we might do 5, 4 and 3 steps (with rests) and that would be enough.

The next time we tried it, we might do 10,9 and 8 steps, and then that was enough. Always with LOTS of rests, lots of yawns, lots of me telling Ozzie he is the best in the world. This is a physical exercise, but it can also be a huge emotional exercise as well, as Ozzie taught me.

It probably took up to a year from when I started until I could actually ask Ozzie to perform the full sequence, without any rests, from 10 down to 1, with Ozzie feeling 100% relaxed with the whole process.

It's a very powerful exercise.

One last thing to note is that the timing of the release is critical. So you need to focus just as much on this as you do on what your horse is doing. You are asking your horse to take four steps backwards. Your horse takes four steps backwards.

Do you release immediately?

Maybe. Maybe not.

You want to release only when your horse has taken four steps backwards, and they are still thinking about going backwards. You'll feel this when you are riding.

Sometimes horses can take steps backwards, but in reality their body is going backwards while their mind is still thinking forwards. So they are moving backwards, but to the rider they still feel like given an opportunity, they would start to walk forwards again.

If you can improve your timing when doing this exercise and only relax and release the horse when they have both stepped backwards AND feel like they are still thinking backwards - that would be perfect.

Lateral movements

Horses can go forwards. Horses can go backwards. Horses can also go sideways. So when we get good at riding forwards and backwards nicely, the next step in both your education and your horse's education is to go sideways.

Any type of sideways movement can also be referred to as a 'lateral' movement.

Sideways movements have many hugely important benefits:

- Sideways movements encourage and teach your horse how to change his posture, in a way that will make it easier for him to carry the weight of a rider.
- Sideways movements encourage your horse to become more athletic, and help your horse to transfer some weight from the forequarters to the hindquarters.
- When your horse begins to transfer some weight from the forequarters to the hindquarters under saddle it decreases the likelihood that being ridden will cause back or physical health issues, particularly in later life. True collection - a goal that nearly all horse riders aspire to - is only possible when there has been a simple transfer of weight from the forequarters to the hindquarters.

When you are riding your horse there are a useful series of sideways exercises you can do to help your horse improve their balance, become more athletic and protect their long term health. I am going to share the first of these exercises with you now.

Note: A common mistake to avoid is to think that to develop collection all you need to do is pull on the reins, so the horse tucks his head in closer to his chest. This is completely incorrect, collection is not a head position. Self- carriage means the horse works in balance and does it by himself.

Shoulder in and out

While most people may have heard of the exercise shoulder in, in fact the very first lateral exercise I recommend you do with your horse is called shoulder out.

Shoulder out is an exercise I like to teach first on the ground and then once the horse and the human understand it we can repeat it in the saddle.

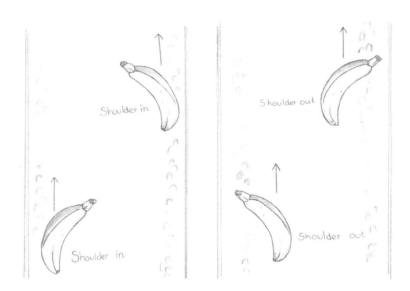

- Imagine the smaller end of the banana is the horse's head.

- You will be asking your horse's body to bend in a similar way to how this banana is bending!
- We are looking for a gentle bend through your horse's whole body - not just in the neck.

Shoulder in and shoulder out are very similar. In shoulder out the horse's head is pointing towards the fence line, with their hindquarters more towards the inside of the arena. In shoulder in the horse's head is pointing towards the inside of the arena, with their hindquarters close to the fence line.

I have some good news for you! You DO NOT need a dressage arena to do this! You can do this on trail rides, along a fence line, on the ground - anywhere you want.

Just by doing this shoulder out exercise you will see a lot of benefits:

- It will improve your horse's balance.
- It will encourage your horse to transfer weight from forequarters to hindquarters.
- It will help your horse become more athletic.
- It will improve your horse's physical posture.
- It is the beginning of collection (which is the most healthy way for a horse to carry the weight of a rider).
- It will help the horse to be able to move and turn with more agility and flexibility.
- When you ride your horse will feel lighter and more responsive to smaller cues.

Now, you might be thinking, do you need some sort of fancy dressage horse to do this? The answer is no. Any horse can do this! From quarter horses and arabs to thoroughbreds, paints and cobs.

We have looked at how you can start this on the ground with your horse. Now it's time to repeat the same exercise in the saddle.

- First we need your horse to have a little energy and to feel relaxed and confident. If your horse has zero energy this is going to be tricky because they will not have enough 'forward'. If your horse is worried or anxious, this is going to be tricky too. You are better off fixing those issues first, before you try shoulder out.
- Next up you will ask your horse to walk along a fence line. You will be very aware that you are looking straight ahead, and not down at your horse's head. This is very important.
- Now walk down the fence line again. This time, you will keep looking straight ahead and now you will ask your horse to create a little bend in their body, by lifting your weight a fraction from the seat bone that is closest to the inside of the arena.
- Make sure your leg which is closest to the inside of the arena is hardly touching your horse at all.
- Finally, move your leg which is closest to the fence line backwards just a fraction to encourage your horse to move his hindquarters a little more towards the middle of the arena.

- Once you get even one step of a sideways movement stop asking your horse to go sideways and walk forwards normally, along the fence line.
- Only ask for one step! Don't get greedy.
- This is an athletic movement you are asking your horse to do, so just ask for a little when you begin.

The Shoulder out exercise

Ride a shoulder out in walk along a fence line. Ask only for 1 step of shoulder in.

Conclusion

Since I was six, I was fascinated by the way horses want to connect with us. At that young age, it seemed almost magical.

How could a mere human truly build trust and partnership with such a large animal who doesn't speak English and has their own free will? And how could I do it in such a way that the horse valued our relationship as much as I did?

My path to finding a way to build that relationship, building on kindness and understanding, has been somewhat of an adventure.

What started as a personal passion ended up becoming one of the world's most loved horse documentaries.

It's not just my journey. Since the Listening to the Horse documentary I've been humbled by the interest of so many horse riders from so many countries around the world, who want to join me in my learning.

The lightness, softness and connection I describe in this book is something that is achievable for all riders. You are good enough. You have the perfect horse.

Because when we are listening to the horse, everything becomes possible.

Congratulations

You finished this book! As an independent author, book reviews are a valuable way for you to help me share this book with the world. If you loved this book, I would be hugely grateful if you could share your review and a photo of this book on your favourite online book store.

Resources

GPS trail riding tracker: www.horsestridesapp.com

Polework Exercises: www.greyponyfilms.com

Horse training tracker: www.rideableapp.com

Dressage lessons: www.dressagehero.com

HORSE BOOKS
by #1 best-selling author
ELAINE HENEY

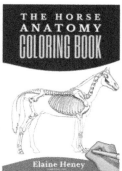

www.elaineheneybooks.com

Made in United States
North Haven, CT
26 February 2023

33142520R00153